# Get Smart!

# MAKE YOUR MONEY COUNT

Lyman MacInnis C.A.

Prentice-Hall Canada Inc., Scarborough, Ontario

**Canadian Cataloguing in Publication Data**

MacInnis, Lyman, 1938-
 Get smart!

Includes index.
ISBN 0-13-354580-6

1. Finance, Personal. 2. Investments. I. Title.
HG179.M32 1983    332.024    C83-098917-X

Prentice-Hall, Inc., Englewood Cliffs, New Jersey
Prentice-Hall International, Inc., London
Prentice-Hall of Australia, Pty., Ltd., Sydney
Prentice-Hall of India Pvt., Ltd., New Delhi
Prentice-Hall of Japan, Inc., Tokyo
Prentice-Hall of Southeast Asia (Pte.) Ltd., Singapore
Editora Prentice-Hall do Brasil Ltda., Rio de Janeiro

ISBN 0-13-354580-6

Production Editor: Catherine G. Leatherdale
Designer: Gail Ferreira
Interior illustrations: Victoria Birta
Production: Alan Terakawa
Composition: ART-U Graphics Ltd.

1 2 3 4 5 6 JD 88 87 86 85 84 83

Printed and bound in Canada by John Deyell Company

# Table of Contents

# Preface

A colleague happened to drop into my office one day while I was working on an early draft of this book. Naturally, we chatted a bit about it, and during the course of our conversation he asked me who would be interested in buying it. I jokingly said "everybody." But then after thinking about it for a time, I realized that my answer was probably right. There *is* something of interest in here for everybody.

When you stop and think about it, managing money in the most appropriate way depends very little on how much of it you have. Whether you have to manage financial affairs carefully just to make it from one payday to the next, or are fortunate enough so that your concern is making the best use of funds available for investment, there are countless considerations in handling money which don't depend on where the decimal point falls.

Of course there are parts of this book that apply only to the person who is faced with making investment decisions. But, there is just as much in here for the person who is doing everything possible just to make ends meet. You will each be surprised at how much of this book applies to both of you. There are chapters ranging from what to do if you win a lottery right up to opening a Swiss bank account.

This book will also be of interest to the many people who, in the course of their everyday activities, advise others on money management. Bank managers, stock brokers, insurance agents, real estate brokers, accountants and lawyers will all find something of interest here. Teachers and students alike, who are interested in money management, will find a lot of resource material in these pages.

The book is written in layman's terms. There is very little technical jargon, and what could not be completely avoided is clearly defined.

Another question my colleague asked me that day was how long it had taken me to write this book. Well, the answer to that question was easy. Over twenty years. Everything that's in this book is based on more than twenty years of experience in helping people manage their financial affairs. The mistakes I haven't made myself, I've seen others make. I think I've seen just about every good and bad financial decision possible, and the results thereof, during that period of time. There are no suggestions in this book that haven't been severely tested many, many times. It doesn't cover every situation, but it deals with the most common and the most important financial decisions that people from all walks of life face.

It is not an income tax book. It is a personal financial management book. Income taxes undeniably form an important part of financial decisions, and in situations where income tax implications are of paramount importance, this book will warn you and suggest you seek specific advice. But, income tax is another subject for other books. Tax implications change every year. The advice and suggestions contained in this book will stand the test of time. So, you can refer to it time and time again and be assured that what's in here still holds true.

There are at least four people to whom I owe a special vote of thanks for the production of this book. Joan Schultz, my secretary and right arm, expertly typed more pages than any human being should ever have to on one subject. Janice Whitford, Acquisitions Editor, and Catherine Leatherdale, Production Editor, of Prentice-Hall, asked all the right questions and made all the right suggestions. My sincere thanks to these three ladies. Thanks, too, to my good friend, David Matheson, Q.C., who first introduced me to the good folks at Prentice-Hall.

# PART ONE

# chapter one

# *Personal Budgeting*

## DISPOSING OF THE MYTHS

Successful personal financial planning begins with budgeting and depends on it as much as the successful operation of a business. Yet even sophisticated business people who wouldn't dream of trying to run their business affairs without a budget will stagger along year after year managing their personal financial affairs on a hit-and-miss basis, avoiding the preparation of a personal or family budget like it was the plague.

This attitude exists because of some myths about personal budgets. Let's dispose of those myths right now.

### Doesn't Cramp Style

A personal budget does not cramp your life style — quite the contrary. By forcing you to realistically appraise your financial situation and allocate available resources on a reasonable basis, the preparation of a personal budget will result in a certain peace of mind throughout the year. With a budget, you know exactly what type of vacation you can afford, when you can trade the car or whether you can have that pool installed.

## No Paper Pollution

Burdensome records need not be kept nor constant comparisons made to the budgeted figures. Actually, the budget itself is the only document you need add to you personal papers. Cancelled cheques, charge card slips, ordinary receipts, and memory (all of which you already have) are the only records required. As for making comparisons with the budget, this need only be done periodically: say, every three months; when you wish to check on a particular item; or when something unexpected necessitates a change in the figures.

## Changes

Here goes another myth. Of course the budget can be changed — and it should be. Whenever a significant change occurs in the amount of cash available, or a major change is required in expenditures, the budget *should* be revised. As a matter of course, many people prepare and revise their budgets on a sliding-year basis. Here is how it works.

Suppose a budget is prepared for a given year and at the end of August it becomes necessary to revise the figures. Don't merely revise the remaining four months of the year. Instead, prepare a new 12-month budget covering the period September to the following August. The merits of this approach are obvious: you will always be reasonably current in your forecasts, you will always have the necessary financial information handy to plan your life style many months ahead (which tends to help avoid financial emergencies), you will find it easier to prepare budgets this way, and you will find it more interesting.

## No Special Skills Required

You do *not* have to be a chartered accountant to prepare a personal budget. By following the suggestions in this chapter, anyone, including older children, can work out a budget. Indeed, the entire family *should* participate in the exercise. Not only does this inspire adherence to the budget by all concerned — after all, *they* helped prepare it, thereby giving tacit agreement to live within it — but having everyone participate in the budget's development establishes an understanding of the family's financial circumstances, and a feeling of responsibility, both of which tend to promote harmony in the home.

One approach which often works well is for each family member (including children) to prepare his or her own budget for items over which he or she has control. Then a budget meeting is held — after dinner some evening — and the individual budgets are consolidated into an overall family budget. In circumstances where some secrecy is in order, the procedure can be tailored to meet those particular needs.

## HOW TO DO IT

A personal budget is really a very uncomplicated thing. Many of us have been brainwashed by the complexity of government budgets and think that doing our own might be almost as difficult. Believe me, it is not. A personal budget consists simply of listing, in an orderly fashion, the amount of money we expect to receive and pay out over the next year, or whatever other period you decide to budget for. It is really a summary of when cash is received and paid out, and for what. That's the basis on which you should prepare it. For example. if you buy furniture for $1,000 to be paid for $100 a month for 10 months, you enter the $100 items, not the $1,000.

Here are a few suggestions for the actual preparation of the budget. The equipment requirements are a couple of sharp pencils and a few sheets of 14-column paper. An adding machine or pocket calculator would be helpful, but they're not necessary.

The first column is used for a description of the items of expected receipts and disbursements. The use of the second column will be described shortly. The next 12 columns will represent the 12 months being budgeted.

Divide the sheet horizontally into two sections. The first few lines, whatever number is necessary, will be used for cash receipts, and the rest of the lines (the second section) will be for cash disbursements. The only exceptions are the first line on the sheet should always be used for cash on hand at the end of the previous month, and the very last line on the sheet will be used for cash on hand at the end of the particular month.

The expected types of receipts and disbursements should be listed on the lines in the first column of the appropriate section.

**FIGURE 1  Sample Budget Sheet**

## PERSONAL BUDGET

| | Total | 19-0 Oct. | Nov. | Dec. | 19-1 Jan. | Feb. | Mar. | Apr. | May | June | July | Aug. | Sept. |
|---|---|---|---|---|---|---|---|---|---|---|---|---|---|
| Balance forward | | | | | | | | | | | | | |
| Salary (net take home) | | | | | | | | | | | | | |
| Family allowance | | | | | | | | | | | | | |
| Investment income | | | | | | | | | | | | | |
| Loans | | | | | | | | | | | | | |
| Other | | | | | | | | | | | | | |
| | | | | | | | | | | | | | |
| Mortgage/Rent | | | | | | | | | | | | | |
| Loan interest and repayments | | | | | | | | | | | | | |
| Property tax | | | | | | | | | | | | | |
| Electricity | | | | | | | | | | | | | |
| Heating | | | | | | | | | | | | | |
| Telephone | | | | | | | | | | | | | |
| Water | | | | | | | | | | | | | |
| Groceries | | | | | | | | | | | | | |
| Maintenance & repairs | | | | | | | | | | | | | |
| Laundry & dry cleaning | | | | | | | | | | | | | |
| Entertainment | | | | | | | | | | | | | |
| Clothing – husband | | | | | | | | | | | | | |
| – wife | | | | | | | | | | | | | |
| – children | | | | | | | | | | | | | |

| Schooling | | | | | | | | | | | | | | | | | | | | | | | |
|---|---|---|---|---|---|---|---|---|---|---|---|---|---|---|---|---|---|---|---|---|---|---|---|
| Medical & dental | | | | | | | | | | | | | | | | | | | | | | | |
| Insurance – life | | | | | | | | | | | | | | | | | | | | | | | |
| – car | | | | | | | | | | | | | | | | | | | | | | | |
| – house | | | | | | | | | | | | | | | | | | | | | | | |
| – other | | | | | | | | | | | | | | | | | | | | | | | |
| Furniture | | | | | | | | | | | | | | | | | | | | | | | |
| Automobile – payments | | | | | | | | | | | | | | | | | | | | | | | |
| – operation | | | | | | | | | | | | | | | | | | | | | | | |
| Subscriptions | | | | | | | | | | | | | | | | | | | | | | | |
| Allowance – husband | | | | | | | | | | | | | | | | | | | | | | | |
| – wife | | | | | | | | | | | | | | | | | | | | | | | |
| – children | | | | | | | | | | | | | | | | | | | | | | | |
| Charities | | | | | | | | | | | | | | | | | | | | | | | |
| Vacation | | | | | | | | | | | | | | | | | | | | | | | |
| Gifts (Xmas, birthday, etc.) | | | | | | | | | | | | | | | | | | | | | | | |
| RRSP | | | | | | | | | | | | | | | | | | | | | | | |
| Emergency fund | | | | | | | | | | | | | | | | | | | | | | | |
| Balance | | | | | | | | | | | | | | | | | | | | | | | |

The appropriate totals for the year should be entered in the second column and then broken down under the respective months in columns 3 to 14. In some cases you will have to fill in column 3 to 14 first in order to arrive at the total for column 2.

Cash receipts are apt to be fixed amounts and should be entered first. When entering disbursements, first enter the *ideal* level of expenditures. Now, the ideal level of expenditures depends on your particular circumstances. Although you often read and hear about "suggested guidelines," such as a particular percentage of income, they are really quite dangerous to rely on. For example, a family of six will spend a lot more on food than a married couple whose children have all grown up and moved out on their own. It costs a lot less for housing in Charlottetown than it does in Toronto. What you should do is go back over your actual expenses for the last few months, adjust for increases in costs and obvious changes in circumstances and start from there. Even a good guess is better than not budgeting at all.

If it turns out that the ideal level of expenditure is unaffordable, you have to re-assess your plans. If you intend to borrow money, the loan proceeds should be reflected in cash receipts. Interest and loan repayments must be provided for in cash disbursements.

The most common error in beginning a personal budget is omitting cash on hand (which should be the first entry in the first month) and unpaid bills at that time (which should be the first entry under disbursements in the first month only — after that they will automatically be included in the relevant disbursement line, but when starting out be sure you don't include them twice).

The next most common error is overlooking disbursements. Don't forget: mortgage or rent payments; groceries; lottery tickets; lunch money; bus fare; laundry; house maintenance and repairs; clothing; furniture; medical, drugs and dental; insurance (life, car, house and other); books, newspapers and periodicals; charitable donations; cable and pay TV; birthdays, anniversaries and weddings; annual payments such as registered retirement savings plan contributions; property taxes; heating; telephone; water; entertainment; school costs; sporting equipment and registration fees for sports; club dues; car operation, licenses and repairs; vacation; and, whenever possible, a little bit for that proverbial rainy day.

# GET YOUR SPOUSE INVOLVED

Regrettably, married women who make their contributions to the family by staying at home to manage the household rather than going out to work — and, indeed, even many who do contribute to the family's earnings — often are not sufficiently involved in managing the family finances.

There is a vast difference between *handling* money (for example, looking after the weekly household budget) and *managing* money (for example, long-term budgeting for the education of children and ultimate retirement resources). Many wives who are quite capable of handling the weekly budget would be completely at sea when faced with long-term management problems. It should not be.

As already mentioned, the financial side of a family's affairs is like that of a business. Income and expense budgets must be considered (regardless of how informal such considerations might be), capital expenditures must be planned and evaluated, and provision must be made for long-term requirements.

These things should all be decided by husband and wife as partners in an enterprise, in every sense of the word. Quite apart from her right to be completely informed of the family's financial affairs and the responsibility to be involved, common sense dictates that every wife be knowledgeable about her family's financial situation. If not, she may find herself in a financial maze when she is least equipped emotionally to cope with it — at the untimely death of her husband. Married people should realize the odds are the husband will die first. As a very minimum a wife should be completely aware of all details regarding wills, insurance, banking, assets and liabilities.

## Wills

Everyone who owns any assets should have a will. It is the only way you can be sure that what you do own will go to the people you want it to, in the manner and when you want it to, should you die. If you don't have a valid will when you die, the government will decide who gets what and when. Even single people with no dependents should have a will, but it is absolutely vital that in a marriage *both* the husband and wife have up-to-date wills.

They both should know where the wills are kept, who the executors are and the exact provisions of each will. Recourse to the courts is scant relief to the wife who discovers after her husband's death that he left everything to a favourite niece — better to thrash that one out now.

A common error is to make a spouse the sole executor of a will. Having him or her as a co-executor with a strong, knowledge-able second party capable of stepping in and taking charge upon the spouse's death is fine, but the surviving partner is usually in no shape emotionally to perform adequately on his or her own as an executor. Don't make a person an executor just because he or she is a fine family friend. That's not doing anyone a favour. Executors should be chosen on the basis of reliability, competence and knowledge of the family and its affairs. Also, don't name your executors without first obtaining their consent and showing them your wills. They many not want to act.

Wills will be covered in more detail in Chapter 2.

## Insurance

Every spouse should know how much insurance his or her partner has, what the payment options are (annuity, lump sum, etc.), which companies the policies are with, the steps required to collect the insurance and, believe it or not, who the beneficiary is.

Instances occur, for example, where the husband was ade-quately covered with insurance but had never gotten around to changing the beneficiary from his mother to his wife. Mother might well see that wife and kiddies are provided for, but might think it best that she continue to control the funds. The courts would sort it out, but better to solve the problem now.

A surviving spouse should also realize that payment of insur-ance is not automatic. Steps must be taken to collect it. A death certificate must be obtained and claims filed. Indeed, only a por-tion of the insurance may be released pending further legal requirements. All these things should be discussed with your insurance agent, the details noted and kept in a safe place.

## Banking

Most people don't realize that upon the instant of death the deceased's bank accounts, including joint accounts, may be frozen and safety deposit boxes sealed. The law, which varies from province to province, allows funds to be released for general purposes with further releases for funeral expenses, etc. The safety deposit box can be opened to remove insurance policies and the will, but other items might remain unavailable until the will is probated.

All of this suggests that both spouses should not only know what bank accounts exist at which branches, and the existence and contents of all safety deposit boxes, but should also know the bank manager's name and how to reach him or her.

Check out what the law is in this respect in your particular province.

### Assets and Liabilities

It seems trite to say that both spouses should be aware of the family's assets and liabilities, but in many cases they are not. It isn't uncommon for investments such as stocks and bonds to languish unnoticed in a secret shoe carton or unknown safety deposit box. It also frequently happens that the surviving spouse is aware of the family assets — house, insurance, etc. — but is completely floored by the discovery of a large broker's margin account and two other bank loans about which only the deceased spouse knew.

### How to Solve the Problem

The solution, of course, is for both spouses to participate in all the financial decisions. One of the best ways to start this is for both spouses to sit down and prepare a list of assets and liabilities, a rough budget for the coming year, and a summary of their wills. You should also prepare a sheet of pertinent data such as the names, addresses and phone numbers of your lawyer, accountant, bank manager, broker and insurance agent, the location of important papers and a description of major assets and liabilities.

The best time to do it is tonight.

## EXAMINE OPTIONS

Although each chapter in this book deals with items that have an impact on family budgeting, the real gains to be made are found in examining your own family's affairs. Every item of expense should be evaluated to determine first, whether it is necessary, and, second, whether there is a more economical way of handling it.

For example, the following are two considerations which are often overlooked when planning one's affairs. The first, whether to lease or buy, is a major consideration which could have a tremendous effect on one's financial well-being; whereas the second, whether to use one of the bank plans for banking, is typical of a small item that could mean a saving of only a few dollars a year. But, every little bit helps. Find 10 ways to save $100 and you're ahead $1,000 per year, which could mean a great deal when put towards, say, an insurance policy or your retirement fund.

## Lease or Buy

Nothing is cheap these days. And as all consumers know, the purchase price of any object — from a toaster to a new car — is only the beginning. The buyer has to reckon with maintenance and service costs. He also has to worry about depreciation. Moreover, ownership involves hidden costs such as insurance and storage space. Bearing this in mind, should you really go out and spend $500 on a carpet cleaner when you could rent it for $20 some weekend? Does it really make sense to buy a car for $12,000 when you could lease it for around $350 a month?

There is no one answer. The decision whether to lease or buy is based as much on emotion as it is on rates of depreciation or utility factors. The point is that almost anything that can be bought can also be leased, whether it be a cactus plant, mobile car telephone, an inflatable tennis court or a $5,000 oil painting for your home or office. The comparison between leasing and buying should always be made, particularly when a big ticket item is involved.

As attractive as the monthly rate may be when compared to a purchase price, there is always the chance that leasing is not the more economical alternative. There is a fairly high mark-up involved in any leased item. Leasing is not for people who can't afford to buy. A person who can't afford to buy an item probably can't afford to lease it either. The exception is, of course, if financing the down payment is the only impediment to being able to afford the object. In fact, to make sure that prospective lessees (that's you, the company you lease from is the lessor) can afford their monthly bills, the major leasing companies issue guidelines on the minimum salary qualifications for their customers.

If you can afford to lease big ticket items, a lease can offer advantages — often in terms of service and, sometimes, in terms of cost. For example, in the case of automobiles, the lessor can usually offer you a saving because he can eliminate the car dealer's mark-up price on new cars, which is often substantial.

That doesn't mean that as the lessee you will automatically realize such savings. Unlike an outright purchase, the true costs of a long-term lease may be hidden in the fine print of a contract. Experienced lessees know that most leasing contracts read as if they were written by a team of lawyers trying to impress the law society. But stripped of legalese, there are basically two types of leases.

## The Operating Lease

The first and more expensive is the operating lease, a typical example of which is a daily car rental. In this kind of arrangement, the company offering the equipment for lease looks after all transactions and maintenance. The lease is usually relatively short-term, is cancellable (normally involving a penalty) and does not include an option to purchase at the end when the lease is up. Most rentals of tools, boats and other equipment needed on a short-term basis, and particularly by individuals, are of this type.

## The Financial Lease

Compared to the operating lease, the second kind of lease — the financial lease — offers less of a service to the lessee. Financial leases are usually long-term (up to 75 or 80 percent of the economic life of the leased item), non-cancellable without the payment of a fairly stiff penalty, and often include an option to purchase or renew at the end of the lease period. This form of lease is generally used for equipment leased by businesses and covers items ranging from typewriters to airplanes.

An individual is most apt to encounter the financial lease as the lessee of a car. Arrangements to lease a car are fairly standard these days. First, the leasing company will want to know what you intend to use the car for — personal or business use — and, if the latter, what kind of business? After that, the car must be chosen — make, model, styling, color and equipment extras. Then a contract will be drawn up.

You should resist the "standard contract." Insist on a contract tailored to suit your circumstances. The key factor in determining the cost will be how much the car is apt to be driven. Taking this into account, and based on the cost of the car to the lessor, the estimated wholesale value of the car at the end of the lease period will be calculated, and a monthly leasing cost established.

The key to making the right decision is whether that cost will be cheaper, overall, than buying the same car.

Let's take a look at a sample lease-buy decision. These aren't real figures — just an example, but they will show you what you must take into account. The list price of the car is $12,000, plus sales tax of, say, 10%. Don't forget the sales tax. So, the total cost is $13,200. If you took out a 15% loan to cover the purchase price, the total cost of the car over two years would be about $15,600. In two years, allowing for depreciation, the car would be worth about $6,000. Assuming that you can obtain that price for the car when you resell it, your net cost of ownership would be $9,600.

If you leased the same car, your monthly rate would vary, depending on the company you leased it from. You should keep in mind the importance of shopping around to obtain the best possible rate. Let's assume you could lease this car for $375 a month plus a tax of 10%. Your total cost of leasing for the two years would be $9,900. So, in this situation, you would be $300 worse off by leasing.

If you have the cash to buy the car, when making the comparison, instead of adding an interest cost to the purchase cost of $13,200, add the after tax interest income you would have received if you invested the money rather than buying the car.

As mentioned, this example is just that — an example. In real life leasing sometimes works out to be cheaper.

If you usually keep a car for three years or more before trading it, you will probably find an outright purchase more economical than leasing. The value of a car depreciates at a much faster rate in the first two years than thereafter. In the above example, the car would probably depreciate $7,000 in the first two years but in its third year, it would, by normal standards, only depreciate a further $1,750. So, if you drive at least 24,000 kilometers a year and trade in your car every two years, leasing may be economical. If you keep your car for three years or more, you will probably be further ahead to purchase it.

These calculations are based on a net lease. Another alternative is the open-end lease. With this type of lease, you agree — in return for a slightly lower monthly rental — to make up the price difference if your car, because of excess mileage, poor maintenance or any other reason, sells for less than the pre-arranged price when the lease expires. You could stand to gain from this type of lease if your car fetches more than the previously set amount.

The lease variations, like others involving maintenance and repair plans, are part of various packages that have developed in the car leasing business since leasing first became popular in the early 60s.

## More Than Cars

As mentioned earlier, almost anything that can be bought can also be leased. Suppose, for instance, that you move from Montreal to Toronto, but you aren't sure how permanent your stay will be. Furniture leasing companies will lease you furniture on a long-term basis with an important option: the lease can be cancelled at any time. Determining how much this privilege costs is difficult because of the discount rates involved in furniture selling. Certainly, if furniture leasing suits your needs, then it would be worthwhile to explore it. But it is not — and is not made out to be — a bargain.

Leasing can be advantageous, however, if you are just starting out in business. One of the most novel alternatives offered in the field is the short-term rental of fully-staffed and equipped offices. There are companies operating in all major cities offering clients very nice office space complete with furniture, telex and copying facilities, a receptionist and secretary, and the use of a boardroom — all for a monthly cost comparable to the salary and fringe benefit costs of one good secretary. The service is used mainly by firms which want to test out new market areas and by individuals who want to start a new business without making a heavy investment in rent and services.

If such a complete package is not required, you can still, of course, rent only what you need. Office furniture, dictating machines, typewriters, telephone answering devices and other equipment can be leased at a cost that works out, over a five-year lease, to be only somewhat higher than the purchase price of the equipment.

You can also rent many other kinds of equipment, such as hand drills, chain saws, garden implements, scaffolding and trailers, on a short-term basis. While the cost compared to the usage time is high, rental firms do offer a definite service. They supply equipment that people use infrequently, have no room to store, or in some cases, no desire to look after. If you rent a $1,000 boat trailer, for instance, it might cost around $30 to $40 per weekend. Still, it may be more economical in the long run than purchasing. The majority of people who buy trailers usually use them very few times in a year. In fact, the trailer often ends up being a storage facility rather than a transportation facility.

Most lease-buy decisions depend on your particular needs. Service, after all, is what most rental and leasing firms are selling, and when it suits your purposes to pay a premium for those services, it makes sense to lease or rent. Otherwise, if you can afford it, you may be better off to buy.

But, *always* consider the alternative leasing versus buying. On complicated and expensive lease decisions, you should shop around until you are satisfied you have the best leasing arrangement possible. Then establish the cost of purchasing the item. Work out the annual depreciation and anticipated maintenance costs involved in ownership over the terms of the proposed lease. Don't forget to add additional financing charges you may incur if you elect to purchase. A comparison of these figures will give you an indication of the real costs involved in either leasing or buying. On a large item, to be absolutely sure, give your accountant a call; there may be important considerations in making the comparison that you've overlooked.

## Should You Join A Bank Plan

Now let's turn attention to a far less significant item in terms of dollars, but one which is indicative of the everyday choices which individuals are faced with. When decisions are made without proper consideration, costs result which could have been easily avoided.

Should you continue to pay a fee each time you use the services offered by your bank, or should you join a bank plan — the package of services offered for a flat fee? Well, like leasing versus buying, it depends.

If you write more than 15 to 20 cheques a month, buy travellers cheques at least once a year, and use a safety deposit box, having a bank plan is probably worth the few dollars a month most of these services cost. (In some cases, it also helps if you tend to run out of cash on the weekend and aren't afraid of using one of the hundreds of tellerless banking units located in many of Canada's urban centres.)

But if you don't fit this profile and still subscribe to a bank service, you're probably subsidizing some of the other subscribers.

Most financial institutions offer customers some form of service package. Yet, while the benefits of each are strikingly similar, there are some differences that could determine which plan you should choose, if you are one of those who could benefit from participating in a plan.

To decide whether a bank service plan is for you, analyze your banking habits. First, do you usually write a lot of cheques?

All the bank service plans offer free, unlimited cheque-writing privileges, and most people with a bank chequing account write at least five cheques a month. But bank plan users should consistently write 15 to 20 cheques a month to benefit from the free chequing privileges of a bank service plan. If you don't, you should make more use of some other part of the plan to compensate for this.

Other services offered by the plans include:

1. overdraft protection;
2. no service charge on money orders or travellers cheques;
3. free utility bill payment;
4. cheque cashing at any branch up to a limited amount, which varies from bank to bank;
5. a reduction on the personal loan rate (in some circumstances); and
6. a reduction in the charge for safety deposit boxes.

## Consider Your Budget Carefully

The point here, though, as in the case of all items on the expense side of your family budget, is to take a look at it and see if there is some way to save some money.

Always remember that an increase of one dollar in your income is reduced by income taxes. But, a decrease of one dollar in your personal expenses is a whole dollar more in your pocket.

## INCOME TAX

Although *now* is always the best time to prepare a family budget and lists of other pertinent financial and personal data, the months of December, January and February seem to be the favourite time for personal financial planning.

This is because December, January and February are the months during which we are constantly reminded of income tax. There's no reason not to make both personal budgeting and income tax planning a year-round consideration. In particular, don't leave your income tax planning until the last minute. Make it a regular part of your continuing personal budgeting process.

Now, this is not an income tax planning book. Rather, it is designed to help you better manage your financial affairs regardless of the level of your income or the amount of taxes you pay. This book will not have to be updated every time the federal government introduces a new tax change, and you can be sure that the advice given here is still valid without having to check to see whether there's been a later edition.

This is not to say, however, that income tax does not represent a major component of everyone's personal financial affairs. Of course it does. And wherever income tax is a significant factor in the advice given in this book, you are reminded to seek professional advice.

If your income tax affairs are particularly complex, you should be seeking professional advice in any event. For those of you whose affairs are less complex, but who want to be sure they are consistent with good tax planning, there is a very easy way to keep up-to-date. All large accounting firms, insurance companies and other financial institutions have up-to-date pamphlets and booklets describing most facets of personal tax planning which they will be pleased to provide you at no cost. Ask for them.

# chapter two

# Some Non-tax Considerations of Estate Planning

As the title suggests, this chapter is not a technical treatment of the many and varied tax considerations surrounding the subject of planning your estate. Indeed, this entire book is devoted to managing your financial affairs in the most appropriate manner, income tax notwithstanding. But like everything fiscal, effective estate planning from an income tax standpoint involves a combination of applying the income tax laws to your particular circumstances, which, for an estate of any appreciable size, should never be undertaken without professional help. This is so for three main reasons: first, no two estates are identical; second, the tax laws in this respect are complex and change frequently; third, there are often other legal considerations, many of which may vary from jurisdiction to jurisdiction.

This chapter *does* discuss considerations which everyone should, and can, bring to bear when planning their estates.

The very essence of estate planning (from the standpoint of what happens when you die) is ensuring that, of what you leave behind, the right things (money included) go to the right people at the right time at the least cost — tax or otherwise.

# PLANNING IS THE KEY

A good estate plan needs the same ingredients as any other successful plan. You have to set your goals, choose the people who are going to advise you and carry out the plan for you, then review it from time to time. Indeed, if you've been following the advice contained in Chapter 1, "Personal Budgeting," you've already taken the first step required to develop an appropriate estate plan — drawing up a statement of assets and liabilities and considering your budget requirements, both long- and short-term.

## Professional Help

At this stage of the game you should call in some help. Throughout this book a lot will be said about getting competent, professional advice and one of the most difficult choices which people have to make from time to time is how to select a professional advisor. What I'm about to say applies, in my view, equally well whether we're talking about choosing an accountant, lawyer, insurance agent or any other professional.

The main point is don't just take the first name you run across or have recommended to you. Even in an emergency you should take the time to consider the three criteria I'm about to lay down. Of course, if it's not an emergency you can be even more selective.

Be sure the person is duly and appropriately qualified in whatever particular field of endeavour you need his or her guidance. There's no point, for example, in going to a chartered accountant whose specialty is computer auditing if your particular problem happens to be an income tax assessment.

Then be sure the particular professional deals with problems the size of yours. There will probably be dissatisfaction all around if you take your house purchase to a lawyer who normally acts only for multi-million dollar shopping centres.

And always remember that the absolutely best criterion possible for the choice of a professional advisor is a personal recommendation from someone whose judgment you trust, who knows the nature of your problem and the type of practice which the professional carries on, and has first-hand knowledge of his or her competence.

Any effective estate plan requires a professional financial advisor and a lawyer to go over your goals with you, advise you on how to best achieve them and actually put your plan into action.

The choice of financial advisor is not an easy one for inexperienced people. Insurance agents, trust companies, accountants, so-called estate planning consultants and sundry others are all called upon from time to time to act in this capacity. About the only thing certain is that there are competent and incompetent estate planners in all these categories. The best basis on which to choose your financial advisor is:

1. obtain referral information; pick someone who has done estate planning work for an acquaintance or comes otherwise highly recommended;
2. stay away from the estate planner who may be trying to sell you something other than his or her professional advice, e.g. insurance, a tax shelter or a shopping centre; and
3. choose someone who has experience dealing with your size of estate.

## Pre-Planning

You can help keep the cost of professional advice at a reasonable level by considering the following *before* you meet with your professional advisors:

1. Prepare that statement of assets and liabilities referred to earlier.
2. Prepare three rough budgets: a current year budget; a long-term budget; and an estimate of how much income your family would need in order to maintain an appropriate standard of living if something happened to you.
3. Consider whether your spouse can adequately manage money. If so, then the suggestions the advisor will make will take a different approach than if your spouse is not sufficiently capable. It's also worthwhile for you to come to grips with this question before meeting with the advisor. There's little point in paying an hourly rate to have the advisor as a spectator at a family quarrel.
4. At what age do you want children to receive money; even if you originally leave everything to your spouse, remember that your spouse should have a will too, and both wills should make provision for the possibility of the two of you dying in a common disaster.

**5.** Are there any special bequests required, e.g. charities, friends, handicapped heirs, etc.

**6.** Who do you want as your executors (more on this shortly).

**7.** Don't let the tax tail wag the family dog.

## WILLS

There is no doubt the single most important ingredient in any estate plan is the will. The simple fact is that every adult should have a will. Married couples should *both* have wills. If only one spouse has a will and they both die in a common disaster, the effect might well be the same as if there was no will at all.

Here are some things to keep in mind so far as wills are concerned.

**1.** Relatively speaking, wills do not cost much. In almost every instance the cost of dying without a will is far greater than the cost of having a will drawn and up-dated from time to time.

**2.** If you die without a will it is unlikely your estate will be distributed in the manner you desire. Provincial law will determine who gets what and when. This could be particularly hard on minor children. A court-appointed official guardian would be a poor choice in comparison to a loving and knowledgeable (from the standpoint of family circumstances) relative or friend.

**3.** The tax cost of dying without a will could be enormous.

**4.** Anytime you make a permanent move from one country or province to another you should have your wills reviewed. This is so because local laws might negate some of the provisions of your will and revisions may be in order. At the very least, you should know the wills are still okay.

**5.** Although you can legally draw your own will, you're a darn fool if you do. Go to a lawyer.

**6.** Having a will may be the only way you can disinherit someone. Even then, the law may overrule you; but again, it's best to know. (Still another reason for having a lawyer draw your will.)

**7.** Review the will with your lawyer any time your circumstances change significantly, and at the very least every five years.

**8.** In most jurisdictions marriage immediately nullifies any existing will, whereas divorce does not.

## Choosing Executors

The executor is the person named in your will who is charged with the responsibility of (and by law given the authority of) carrying out the provisions of your will.

As someone once suggested, the perfect executor would be a tactful, diplomatic, loving family member who is both a lawyer and a chartered accountant with a wide background in investing, and who will live forever. Well, let's see who's second best. Here are some things to remember:

1. Pick someone who is honest. Remember that your executor has, at least for a period of time, complete control over your estate and its assets.
2. Your executor should know you and your family and live in the same area. Heirs in Vancouver and an executor in St. John's add up to bad news.
3. Pick someone who has a solid knowledge of, or access to, business and financial management.
4. Always check with your choice before actually naming him or her to determine if they are willing to act, and more important, if they will have the time to do so.
5. Show them a copy of your will. There might be some provision in there they would not be comfortable with, such as complete discretion as to whether a recalcitrant teenager ever inherits anything, or a direction to cremate your remains which your executor might object to on religious grounds.
6. You probably should name a team of executors — say, your spouse and lawyer or accountant. Also, you should provide for an alternate executor in the event either of the named executor can't or won't act.

## QUESTIONNAIRE

Appendix A is a sample questionnaire which I use as a starting point in planning a person's financial affairs. It is reproduced at the back of the book as an example of the various questions and type of data that must be carefully considered in formulating any estate plan. Of course, the questionnaire is designed to cover a wide range of personal situations and any particular person would be unlikely to have to answer all the questions or use all the schedules.

Why not use it now as a record of your affairs. It's very thought provoking. Not only that, but it's a very useful document to have for the following reasons. It will provide you with a record, in one place, of all relevant personal financial information. This will allow you to better assess your current situation and will make up-dating the data a lot easier. It will also be an excellent starting point (and money saver) should you decide to engage a professional advisor. It would be of particular interest to the executor of your will. As a matter of fact, it should be treated with the same respect as other important documents, such as wills. Keep a copy handy for easy reference, but also have a copy in safekeeping, such as with your lawyer or in a safety deposit box. Remember, though, when you up-date, up-date all copies.

## chapter three

# *The Ten Most Common Personal Financial Planning Mistakes*

## THE LIST, IN ORDER

Over the past twenty years I've seen just about every mistake that a person can make in personal financial planning. Some of them I made myself — and that's the best teacher of all.

As a result, I've compiled a list of what, in my opinion, are the ten most common personal financial planning mistakes. By "most common" I mean those that are made most often by most people. And that's the order in which I'll present them here — the order of frequency, not the order of devastation.

Another thing about these mistakes is that people at all levels of wealth make them: these are the same mistakes that cause financial difficulties for the millionaire and labourer alike, the only difference being in the number of zeroes in the sums involved. So, whether you're a person who rarely makes it from payday to payday or a multi-millionaire, the following are the mistakes to avoid:

### Number One

There's no doubt whatsoever in my mind as to what the most common financial planning mistake made by most people, most often, is. It's: *buying too much on credit!* I've seen more people, rich and poor alike, get into financial difficulty because of buying too much on credit than for any other reason. Now, the key words here are "*too much*". It's a rare person indeed who never has to borrow or buy on credit. But, don't overdo it. A good rule of thumb is to only borrow for what you *need*. Wait until you have cash for the things you simply *want*. Why? Because buying on credit often doubles and triples the cost by the time you pay it off.

### Number Two

Mistake number two is *borrowing at the wrong place.* I should explain quickly what I mean by this. I'm not suggesting one institution is better than another. What I am saying is if you *must* borrow, then borrow where you get the best interest rate, all other things being equal. Let's take an example. Suppose you're going to have to borrow five thousand dollars for a car, and you intend to pay it off over three years. How much difference would it make if you borrowed the money at, say, 10% rather than from another source at, say, 15%. Well over the three years it would be a difference of over $400 — tax-free.

### Number Three

Mistake number three is *not paying off debts as quickly as possible*, particularly charge accounts and credit card balances, where people often forget that if you don't pay off those balances *in full* every month, it's the same as borrowing at very high interest rates. In my opinion you should pay off your mortgage as fast as you can, too. Another example, if you paid off a 15%, $50,000 mortgage over fifteen years rather than twenty-five years, how much do you think you would save? Well, you would save about $70,000!

### Number Four

In my opinion, the fourth most common personal financial planning mistake that people make, is *renting living accommodation* rather than buying it.

Now, hold it! Don't get upset yet! I know there are lots of people who would far rather rent than own, and that's a personal decision I'd never try to argue anyone out of. With rent controls and high interest rates, you might even be better off in the short haul renting rather than owning.

But, from an economic standpoint, over the long-term, I think it is a personal financial planning mistake to rent rather than own your living accommodation.

There are several factors backing this opinion: first of all, your home is the only investment you can sell for a profit and get an income tax break on. Second, it's about as good a hedge against inflation as you'll find anywhere — especially over the long-term. Third, it is one of the very few investments you can make that also fills an absolute need. As mentioned in Chapter 11, everybody needs a roof, four walls, and a place to go to the bathroom. And last, but certainly not least, because I think this is often the most overlooked factor — your own home provides more potential for continuous enjoyment than almost any other investment possible.

### Number Five

*Not budgeting for once-a-year expenditures* such as insurance, vacations, subscriptions, and even Christmas, constitutes mistake number five.

### Number Six

*Not budgeting at all.* See Chapter One.

Most people shy away from personal budgets because they think they have to be very formal and have the effect of hamstringing their activity. Nothing could be further from the truth. Personal budgeting simply involves sitting down and comparing your planned expenses with your income over, say, the next year. It will help you decide what you can afford — and when — thereby cutting down on interest expense. Everyone I know who has tried personal budgeting has found that it gives them greater financial freedom, not restricted them.

### Number Seven

Mistake number seven is *neglecting to comparison shop.* Now, I don't mean you should burn two dollars worth of gas to save thirty cents on a jar of peanut butter. I'm referring to big ticket items like cars, furniture, jewellery, registered retirement savings plans and the like. And remember that this cuts both ways. On big ticket, capital goods that you expect to own and use for a long period of time, the most expensive, quality item is very often the cheapest in the long run. It is a fact that a four-hundred-dollar suit will last longer than two two-hundred-dollar suits.

### Number Eight

Mistake number eight is: when investing, *trying to make a quick buck* instead of going for a lower, but surer, return. If you're faced with two investment choices and the rate of return on one is double that of the other, the reason is that the chance of losing your money if you invest in the one with the higher rate is a lot greater than if you go for the more conservative investment.

### Number Nine

Mistake number nine — and, this is a fairly recent one, much more prevalent in recent years than earlier — is *making investments that you can't really afford,* such as borrowing to buy stocks. Increases in interest rates, drops in the market and the need to get your cash back for other purposes can all force you into panic moves, causing you to sell at a loss, whereas if you could really afford the investment you could weather the storm.

### Number Ten

Mistake number ten is: *thinking the future will take care of itself.* It never has and it never will. We have to plan prudently for long-term things like our children's education and our retirement. We should also defend as well as we can against emergencies such as the death of the breadwinner, collapse of a business, run-away inflation and high interest rates. As a matter of fact, a little more self-reliance may be just the economic tonic this country needs.

## WHAT CAUSES THESE MISTAKES

I've just given you my list of what I think the ten most common personal financial planning mistakes are. Now, a few words about what, in my opinion, causes people to *make* personal financial planning mistakes.

There are as many causes, I suppose, as there are people, and some can't be avoided. But, I think I can categorize the avoidable ones under the following headings.

Trying to keep up with the Joneses: this drives many, many people into life styles which they simply can't maintain in the long-run and then the mistakes start to compound.

Thinking that the world owes you something: this person tends to sit back and wait for someone — probably the government — to bail him or her out. In the meantime others are fending for themselves and outstripping the laggard.

Trying to get something for nothing, or listening to the "buddy have I got a deal for you" line: there never has been, there isn't now, and there probably never will be, such a thing as a free lunch.

Thinking the future will take care of itself: this is not only one of the causes, it's one of the mistakes, too. What we do today determines in large measure what will happen to us tomorrow.

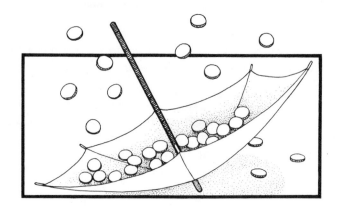

# chapter four
# *Tax Shelters*

It should be made abundantly clear right now that the income tax shelters that are dealt with in this chapter are the likes of films, natural resource deals, and real estate shelters such as multi-unit residential buildings (MURBs). This chapter's comments do not apply to registered retirement savings plans (which are dealt with in the next chapter) nor to other so-called "statutory" plans (such as employee pension plans) which are beyond the scope of this book.

Tax shelters come and tax shelters go, depending on the most part on the whims of successive Finance Ministers. About the only thing consistent about the various tax shelters that have come and gone in recent years is the wake of unhappy people left behind — people who lost money, even after the tax break.

Therein lies the secret of investing in tax shelters. If the particular deal — whether it be a real estate development, a movie, television show, or an oilwell — needs the tax break to make it viable, then don't go for it. On the other hand, if the tax break only makes the return on investment better, then it makes some sense. There's precious little to be said for getting a fifty-cent tax refund because you lost a dollar.

Never invest in a tax shelter without first obtaining professional advice regarding both the tax implications and the investment attributes of the deal. And always be sure you get your own independent advice; don't rely on the promoter's advisors.

One question which you should always obtain an acceptable, reasonable answer to before investing in a tax shelter that's being offered to the public is: why are the industry people (the insiders) not investing in this, why is it being offered to the public? As one commentator put it, "No one was around trying to get me to invest in the movie *E.T.*, but I had lots of opportunity to invest in *The Day That the Sheep Stood Still*."

Another problem with tax shelters that rely on the tax break to provide a reasonable rate of return is that tax laws change, and sometimes with retroactive effect. Still another problem is that as a rule tax shelter investments are often very hard to dispose of. In many instances the tax break is only available to the first investor. In others, the very existence of the tax shelter causes a glut on the market.

These cautionary comments do not apply to some of the statutory tax shelters such as registered retirement savings plans, registered pension plans, deferred profit sharing plans and the like. In almost all cases these retirement-oriented tax shelters should be taken advantage of to the maximum extent. But like all things connected with income tax, you must make sure that you are completely familiar with the provisions as they apply to you. The general application may be fine, but in your particular circumstances there may be some exception. So, always get professional advice and guidance.

# chapter five

# *A Consumers' Guide to RRSPs*

## GENERAL CONSIDERATIONS

Each year, thousands of Canadians rush out to enroll in a registered retirement savings plan. While well-informed of the tax savings obtainable through an RRSP, they find the variety of plans available confusing and, in many cases, choose plans unsuited to their ages or to their financial situations.

Indeed, with banks, trust companies, brokerage houses, mutual funds, insurance companies and credit unions all busy trying to attract potential shoppers to the hundreds of plans they offer, it's no wonder many people would prefer to leave the choice to an expert. Still, most people lack the necessary knowledge or advice when making their commitment. Yet even if you're not an expert or not in contact with one, there are steps you can take to ensure that you get the best possible plan to suit your financial situation.

With or without professional help, you must consider three important questions before buying:

**1.** How flexible should the plan be to meet your financial needs in case of an emergency?

**2.** How much risk are you willing to accept as a trade-off for a high rate of return?

**3.** Which plans are the most compatible with your savings and other investments?

The ease with which payments can be made without following a rigid schedule is extremely important in any plan. You must consider whether you will be able to commit a continuing fixed annual or monthly amount to an RRSP. This becomes extremely important in plans offered by life insurance companies which may require sustained payments over the life of an RRSP.

You should be aware that with such plans, substantial portions of early payments often go to cover commissions and administrative costs. An investor, forced by an emergency to withdraw funds early in the plan's life, could find the first year's payment gone. Most investors should avoid plans that commit them to following rigid deposit schedules and, instead, choose one or more of the other types of RRSPs available that allow contributions anytime at no fixed rate and withdrawals without a major penalty.

The second point investors should consider is risk. In the context of investment plans, risk describes the range in rates of return you might expect from different types of plans. Guaranteed plans carry the least risk. With these plans you know in advance how much can be earned over a specified period, which could be anywhere from a few months or many years. Depending on the issuer and the length of the time, rates are usually one or two points below current interest rates.

At the opposite end of the spectrum are the equity funds whose returns are based on stock market activity. In theory, these could give a higher rate of return than other types of RRSPs over the long term, if the value of the underlying stocks in the plan's portfolio grows.

But, not all equity-based funds perform equally. For example, over a three-year period, the average annual compound rate of return for equity funds eligible for RRSPs might be 12%. Yet several would likely earn in excess of 20%, while a few might earn less than 5% annually. Some might lose. Over a long-term, however, equity funds, on average, probably return less to investors than the guaranteed funds.

Clearly, stocks are not the best investments for all economic periods. In fact, the best performing RRSPs during periods of high inflation are guaranteed plans.

Because of the wide swings possible in equity fund performance, they should not be considered by people approaching retirement age. They are best suited to taxpayers who can look at a 20-year, or longer, time span and who are not bothered by fluctuations of stock markets. Indeed, equity fund RRSPs should be avoided by people who may be forced to liquidate their plan prematurely.

The third type of fund, called the fixed income fund, is invested in bonds, mortgages or both. It is most suitable for individuals who are willing to accept some volatility in rate of return in order to get greater long-term gains, and who are unwilling to accept the extreme volatility of equity funds. More experienced investors often spread their money among different types of funds, trading off expected return for a reduction of risk.

Remember, the rate of return you earn on your RRSP determines in large part the amount of money you will collect at retirement. An individual who contributes $3,500 annually to a plan for 30 years and earns an average rate of 5%, compounded annually, would accumulate $199,317. If that same individual were able to earn an average return of 7% on annual contributions, $283,382 would be available at retirement time. An average return of 9% would result in a total of $408,923 while an average return of 11% would provide $597,063. It's easy to understand why many individuals choose the higher risk funds even though they have proved poor investments during some periods.

Even small investors who are able to set aside, say, $1,000 a year, should spread the risk. They would be wise to split their contributions between two plans of the same type. By diversifying you reduce the possibility of investing everything in a plan that may not perform as well as others.


# EQUITY PLANS

Equity, or stock-based, registered retirement savings plans may give you the greatest potential return for your investment — but at the highest risk.

Certainly, the risk factor in these plans was most prevalent in the early 1980s when the roller coaster performance of the stock market saw many investors scurrying to get their nest egg to a safer place.

But if you are not upset when the stock market takes a nose-dive, and if you can take a long-term outlook for investment, equity funds can be rewarding. Even during a period of mediocre market performance, for instance, some equity-based plans outperformed their more sedate relatives. But, a lot didn't.

Equity funds, as a group, perform better than fixed income or guaranteed funds in periods of low inflation.

For investors willing to gamble on this scenario, there is a bundle of equity-based plans on the market. Banks, trust and insurance companies all sell equity funds. Stock and mutual fund brokers also offer these RRSP alternatives. Even a couple of department stores have entered the field by offering a series of house brand funds, some of which are eligible as RRSPs. Keep in mind that not all mutual funds sold in Canada are eligible for retirement plans; the fund's prospectus will inform you if the units qualify for RRSPs.

Fund performances vary widely. The majority of funds have had a performance close to the market average with few either greatly outperforming or underperforming the index.

If more than one ending date is considered for measurement, the results suggest that few funds consistently outperform or underperform the market in either rising or falling periods. Of those that are consistently at either end of the performance spectrum, superior or inferior results are usually attributed to the decisions of a single individual. It is exceptional for a fund to disclose to investors the people responsible for deciding what stocks are bought and sold for the portfolio. In many cases, it's a committee that makes the investment decisions; rarely has a committee outperformed the market.

Because of this, the majority of equity funds will have, over time, returns comparable to those of the indexes. The reason is relatively simple: most fund management committees try to determine which industry groups or stocks will outperform the market, and which will not. They reach a consensus and buy and sell stocks to fit the model they've created, usually based on a stock market index.

However, most other fund management groups would act in a similar fashion and, because they all use the same type of brokers' reports and attend the same meetings, it's no surprise that results don't differ substantially from group to group. And because these fund managers' decisions represent a high percentage of the trading on stock markets, the results of professional management and general stock market performance are similar.

Most fund managers are unwilling to load their portfolios with high-risk stocks because this strategy proves unprofitable during a period of volatile stock market performance. A more common strategy is to increase or decrease the portion of the portfolio held in cash according to the manager's expectations of the market's direction. Again, because most institutional managers use similar information in arriving at their decisions, this strategy also seldom leads to consistently superior performances.

A handful of fund managers have been able to outperform their competition. They've done this by ignoring the performance of the markets as the basis for their portfolio holdings. Rather, they have been bold enough to concentrate the bulk of holdings in stocks or industry groups which they believe to be the most undervalued. Such a strategy might lead to buying a holding of, say, 50% oil shares during a time when these are out of favour, then switching out of these into cash or another industry group as oil stocks' value comes back.

Managers who are agile enough to use this type of portfolio strategy usually show positive results even in periods when the market falls. The problem facing investors is that this type of manager is scarce. The best investors can expect is to sort through the funds' results and spread their money among two or three equity funds that appear more often than not among the better performers.

If you are still committed to investing in this area, your first step should be to examine past performance records. The historical results of fund management cannot be used to predict future performance with any degree of accuracy. However, the small investor has few other indicators available. His account is not large enough to demand detailed information about portfolio managers' experience, size of analytical staffs, or investment strategies. Such information is readily available only to large multi-million dollar corporate or union pension funds. But, if it's any consolation, these large investors obtain results comparable to the small investor's.

In using historical records, begin by rejecting any fund which consistently ranks below the average performance of the group.

Once you've narrowed your choice to funds which usually match or beat market performance, examine the size of the fund. Be suspicious of top performing funds with only a few hundred thousand dollars of assets. Many fund managers have been unable to sustain top performance once their funds grow into millions; the result is that the larger size has forced them to broaden their choice of stocks, leading to a respectable, but average, performance. Also examine the fund's investment objectives to make sure the fund's objectives are compatible with yours.

When you've narrowed the field down to a handful, it's time to compare costs including registration and redemption fees, if any. Published performance figures tell only part of the story. Beware of funds having high sales charges or front-end loads. If you invest in these funds, out of every dollar you contribute, as little as ninety cents may be invested on your behalf. In most cases, a sales charge does not even assure superior performance. But if you are interested in specific funds that can only be purchased through a sales agent, determine if the commission is negotiable. The growth of trust company funds, which are generally sold without charges, has caused many mutual fund operators and brokers to be flexible about front-end loads. In some instances it's possible to bargain for a lower rate.

If you are unwilling or unable to investigate the various equity RRSPs available, probably your best bet lies with some of the no-load or low-load funds sold by trust companies. While these funds are not usually among the top performers, they also seem to avoid the bottom.

Any equity fund RRSP, almost by definition, offers diversification by spreading your money among many different stocks. Even so, it's best not to gamble that any single manager will give consistently superior performance. Rather, spread your retirement savings among two or three funds. This way you lower the chance of having all your money with one manager, who for one reason or other, may not keep up with the competition.

## SELF-DIRECTED PLANS

Self-directed registered retirement savings plans allow you to make all the investment decisions. The plans can be tailor-made to suit your whims, needs, preferences and hunches. Indeed, a self-directed plan can be as risky as you make it. Properly managed, it can offer rewards exceeding those of institutionally managed RRSPs. However, most self-directed programs are usually mismanaged, resulting in poor returns.

The major advantage of self-directed plans for sophisticated investors is that they allow concentration in certain types of investment, such as high-yield mortgages, unavailable in institutional funds. Self-directed plans allow stock investors flexibility to quickly change industry groups or switch to cash.

A self-directed plan requires some investment sophistication and should be considered as an alternative to professionally managed funds only by individuals with a good knowledge of some of the investment alternatives that qualify for inclusion in the plan.

Of course, investors can always retain investment counsel to manage their self-directed plans, but this is an additional expense, and is no guarantee of superior performance.

Setting up a self-directed plan is relatively simple. The arrangements have to be made through an institution which acts as administrator and trustee. It accepts your deposits and receives or delivers any securities you may have bought or sold.

The cost of enrolling in a self-directed plan are relatively high compared to other types of RRSPs because of the extensive administrative work needed. And charges vary widely among the companies that offer them.

There may also be additional charges for each transaction depending on the particular company's arrangement. For small amounts in a fund — say under $10,000 — the costs of administering a self-directed RRSP may erode any advantage of using such a plan.

Keep in mind when you engage in such a plan that there is a penalty for holding an investment that becomes non-qualified. For example, a stock may come under this category if the company moves outside Canada, becomes private, or its shares are exchanged for non-qualified securities as in some mergers. For as long as such a security is held (with a few exceptions) the plan is subject to a pretty hefty tax penalty.

Most individuals who take out self-directed RRSPs do so because they expect to earn a higher return than that available with managed funds. They expect to do this either through their own idea of having superior knowledge or the expert advice of their advisors.

Some succeed. Many, however, fail.

The successful ones have a number of things in common: they usually concentrate in certain types of securities that are not found in large portions in institutionally-managed funds; they are diversified but not overly so; they contain some relatively high-risk securities.

However, in the case of stocks, the higher risk with a self-directed plan is partially off-set by the plan's greater flexibility. The small size of these plans, relative to the multi-million dollar pooled funds, allows sophisticated investors to switch the portfolio mix at will.

A popular stock strategy is to concentrate stocks in specific industries in the expectation that such industry groups will greatly outperform the whole market. Success using this strategy depends on how able you are in selling and switching to other investments or holding cash. Many investors who attempt this strategy fail because they put all their money in too few stocks. Or they depend on the same brokers' advice which is available to every other player in the market.

The minimum amount needed to justify a self-directed plan really depends on the type of securities mix an individual wants in an RRSP portfolio. For stocks, probably enough diversification can be built into a portfolio worth $20,000. For mortgages, the amount needed for diversification may be in the $30,000 to $50,000 range; some experts use substantially higher figures. The mortgages do not have to be owned by one individual but can be held by several parties.

While in theory small portions of mortgages, say only a couple of thousand dollars, could be placed in a self-directed RRSP, in practice, most of the mortgage brokers, accountants and lawyers who deal in mortgages don't like dividing them into such small amounts because of the administrative costs involved in servicing the interests. Many prefer minimum interests in the $30,000 to $50,000 range and up.

You should not dabble in a self-directed RRSP without familiarizing yourself with the income tax rules affecting RRSPs. In particular you have to be completely familiar with which investments qualify and which don't.

The main disadvantage of a self-directed RRSP is if you get wiped out you have no one to blame but yourself.

# FIXED INCOME FUNDS

Fixed income registered retirement savings plans provide a middle of the road alternative to guaranteed RRSPs and equity-based plans. By relying on investments in the bond and mortgage markets which are more stable than the stock market, fixed income RRSPs provide an excellent balance between higher risk equity-based plans and the very secure guaranteed funds.

Indeed, during periods of high but stable interest rates, when the growth rate of inflation is relatively constant, fixed income RRSPs can be consistently good performers. Although they do poorly during periods when inflation and interest rates are rising, they perform well when both inflation and interest rates are falling.

Fixed income funds are alternatives for individuals who are unwilling to accept the broad variations in rates of return that come with owning a stock-based plan. They are worthwhile investments if you are willing to shoulder some fluctuation in value over time as a trade-off for a better return than guaranteed RRSPs deliver.

In effect, the investor buys units in the fund, becoming a part owner of the bonds and mortgages in the portfolio. The financial institution charges a management fee, usually a percentage of the value of the account; any profits or losses are charged to the fund. This differs from guaranteed RRSPs in which investors lend the institution their money for a fixed term at a fixed interest rate. Fixed income funds are available through most financial institutions and many mutual fund dealers.

Units in a fixed income fund are valued at the total worth of the portfolio divided by the number of units outstanding. The number of units changes as new contributors invest in the fund or others redeem their units. And the value of any bond or mortgage fund unit changes with variations in interest rates. If rates rise, the value of outstanding bonds or mortgages falls and if interest rates decline, the market value of the portfolios goes up.

Unit prices of fixed income funds move in a similar manner because each fund unit represents part ownership in a portfolio which may contain hundreds of bonds or mortgages that can differ from each other in quality, coupon rate and term to maturity. Each shift in interest rates or change in demand for bonds of specific quality or term will increase or decrease the value of the total portfolio and, in turn, affect the price of a unit of the fund.

Depending on the type of financial institution managing the portfolio, fund values are calculated on a daily, weekly or monthly basis.

The rate of return earned on a fixed income fund depends largely on how the manager structures different types of bonds and mortgages in the portfolio.

Because of these higher yields, during a period of low inflation a portfolio with a lot of long-term bonds would have a higher return than one with shorter maturities. But even in bond and mortgage portfolios, high return securities can mean higher risk. If interest rates rise, the fund with the longer maturities would fall in value more than one with a portfolio of shorter maturities.

The shorter bonds, while yielding less, are not as volatile because the date of maturity, when money can be re-invested, is closer. Consequently, a bond manager expecting interest rates to be stable over a long period would include in his portfolio a heavy weighting of high coupon, long-term bonds to maximize his fund's income.

Bonds issued when interest rates were lower than today's, trade at a discount from their issue price. If a manager expects interest rates to remain stable for a long period, he will not usually hold large amounts of such bonds in his portfolios. Instead, he will buy high coupon bonds which provide high current income now as opposed to a low current income from discount bonds and a large lump sum gain at maturity. He would do this because the additional income can be re-invested, giving the fund additional revenues. But if a manager expects a substantial drop in rates over a short period, he may switch to discount bonds and improve the fund's short-term performance.

If a manager is correct in anticipating the timing and direction of interest rate swings, he can increase his fund's performance substantially. But if he is wrong, his error in judgment could prove costly to his fund investors.

Mortgages usually pay a higher rate of return than bonds. However, there has been little difference in performance, historically, between well-managed bond funds and well-managed mortgage funds. The trading flexibility a bond fund manager has relative to poorly marketable mortgages offsets the higher interest rates usually available from mortgages.

Because of the similarity in returns, cost should be given major consideration along with the fund's historical performance when choosing a fixed income RRSP.

Here are some steps to follow.

First, narrow your choice by eliminating any fund which consistently ranks below the average performance of the group. While this judgment should be made on as long a term basis as possible, some funds have only been in existence a few years and should not be eliminated for this reason alone.

Second, examine the size of the fund. Be suspicious of top performing funds with only a few hundred thousand dollars of assets. The managers of such funds might not be able to sustain top performance if the funds' characteristics change through growth.

Once you've narrowed the field down to a handful or two, it's time to shop for cost. Registration, administration and withdrawal fees vary widely among institutions. These charges can make a substantial difference on your overall return.

And before you buy, remember the old saying about putting all your eggs in one basket. It's best to hold your retirement savings in more than one fixed-income RRSP to reduce the risk of having all your retirement savings with a manager whose luck or judgment turns bad.

## GUARANTEED FUNDS

Guaranteed registered retirement savings plans offer the most security. Indeed, they are the only plans that should be considered by most individuals approaching retirement age. In fact, anyone in his or her mid-50s or up, whose retirement nest egg is locked into RRSPs, should be in this type of plan. They are also suitable for individuals who are unwilling to assume the risks that come with owning units in equity and fixed income RRSPs.

With a guaranteed plan, a financial institution contracts to pay you a specified rate of interest for a specified period of time. After that term expires, the rate paid can be revised up or down to a new level which remains in effect for an additional period. Depending on the fund, this rate might be guaranteed from one month to five years.

In effect, you are lending a bank, trust company or other financial institution your money for a specified time. The institution, in turn, agrees to guarantee you a given rate of interest whether or not they make a profit by re-lending your funds. The advantage to you is knowing in advance that at the end of the period, without risk, the value of your RRSP will be the principal amount in the plan at the beginning plus interest on that amount at the guaranteed rate of return by the institution.

But you will pay a price for this security. You can usually expect to earn between one or two percentage points below the prevailing mortgage rate; the difference becomes the institution's markup. Still, this sacrifice of higher return in exchange for security is essential for many people.

There is usually a choice between two types of guaranteed plans. One is in many ways similar to a bank account with chequing privileges. This type of plan — a special savings account — can be pulled out anytime without any major penalty. The interest rates paid are relatively low. Interest rates paid in savings account RRSPs are guaranteed for fairly short periods — as little as one month and as long as six months — depending on the issuer.

These types of RRSPs are the most flexible, as far as withdrawals are concerned and, because rates can change often, they are the quickest to reflect changes in interest rates. They are the most suitable plans for individuals within five years of retirement or for anyone who doesn't want to be locked into a plan for an extended period.

Savings account RRSPs are also used by individuals who believe that the trend of interest rates is up. These plans are among the best performers of all types of RRSPs during such a scenario. For those who believe rates will rise during the short-term, savings account RRSPs can be used as a temporary haven and later switched to a guaranteed plan with a lock-in period or to a fixed income or equity RRSP.

The other type of guaranteed RRSP, a guaranteed investment certificate RRSP, requires that you agree to leave money deposited for a term of one to five years. This allows the institution to re-lend your money with some knowledge as to how long it will have the use of your funds. For instance, if money is deposited with a trust company which guarantees interest rates for five years, then the trust company can re-lend that money also for a five-year period.

Even so, you can pull your money out of most plans before five years is completed if an emergency develops, but be prepared to pay a penalty in the form of a substantial reduction in interest received.

People who invest in plans with long lock-ins when inflation is high get better rates than people who invest when inflation is on the downswing. Over the past few years, interest rates in Canada have been volatile but have remained near historically high levels. Indeed, guaranteed funds have had enviable performance records and have attracted many investors who, in previous years, put their money into equity funds.

Regardless of whether you choose a guaranteed savings account RRSP or one with a lock-in period you can save money by shopping around and matching a plan to your own situation. Interest rates, as well as registration, administration and withdrawal fees, vary widely among institutions. And don't just look at interest rates. Fees charges can make a difference on your overall return.

For instance, a guaranteed savings account available from one trust company offered a 10½% interest rate for six months. This fund had no other administrative or withdrawal fees. A second trust company guaranteed 11%, also for six months, but charged a 1% withdrawal penalty up to $100 when the plan was terminated. The first plan is the better investment for individuals who have less than $20,000 accumulated when they close their RRSP. For larger amounts, the second plan is preferable.

Another point to consider in choosing a guaranteed RRSP is the frequency of interest compounding. This is important because it can affect the return you can receive. For instance, an institution offering 8½% compounded annually would pay $85 interest on principal of $1,000 at the end of one year. One offering 8½% compounded semi-annually would pay $42.50 interest after six months and an additional 4¼% on $1,042.50 — about $44.13 — six months after that.

Compounding semi-annually has the effect of raising the return to about 8.68%. Although the increased return seems small, the difference between annual and semi-annual compounding can be tremendous over the life of your RRSP. A few financial institutions even compound interest quarterly and others monthly, so it pays to shop around.

## THE INSURANCE RRSP

By any measure, cash value life insurance policies make poor registered retirement savings plans. Indeed, such plans fail in the most critical areas of plan selection: flexibility and rate of return relative to risk. They are also, when registered as RRSPs, an expensive way of buying life insurance.

Failure to keep up premiums on these policies could lead to their cancellation and the loss of insurance coverage which may not be easily replaced. It is under such circumstances that investors discover what poor investments they have chosen. Usually, people learn to their chagrin that they don't even get back all their investment. In fact, in the early life of such plans, it is common for the cash surrender value to be nil.

This is because early deposits go to cover non-refundable commissions and administration costs. Consequently, people who decide to switch plans find that they have paid a heavy penalty for not investigating.

Tax laws allow the cash surrender portion — the so-called savings element — of life insurance policies to be registered as RRSPs. As a result, many Canadians buy these plans in the belief they are providing their families with adequate insurance coverage and themselves with good retirement savings plans. These investors fail to realize that these plans were designed to provide life insurance, not to be cashed in for retirement savings.

The worst possible insurance RRSP alternatives are ones involving the registration of whole life insurance policies. Ordinary whole life policies require the payment of premiums every year for life in order to keep the death benefit provisions in effect. Limited pay life policies are similar, except that the premium period is limited to a specific time, usually the age at which the policy holder expects to retire. With both types of policies, the insurance benefit is paid at death.

However, tax laws require RRSPs to be terminated when you reach a certain age (71 at the time of writing), but by doing that you cancel your policy and may lose the insurance benefit. Indeed, you may have paid expensive whole or limited pay life premiums for coverage which expires at age 71 — and received a return on your savings as little as half that of guaranteed plans.

A third type, endowment insurance, is the only one designed to mature and pay a benefit during policyholders' lives. These once popular policies have fallen from favour as investors have realized that low rates of return make them an expensive way of saving money.

Investors who want a combination of life insurance and retirement savings are probably better off getting term insurance in the amount they need to suit their individual requirements and then choosing an RRSP to accommodate their financial situation and age.

Such a strategy has several advantages, the most important being a high degree of flexibility in making deposits into the RRSP. Also important is the cost of the insurance element. Term insurance is relatively inexpensive for younger men and women and allows them to purchase large amounts of coverage when it is most needed. Like RRSPs, costs of insurance vary widely among companies so it pays to shop around for coverage.

## WHEN IN DOUBT

If you have any doubt about the type of registered retirement savings plan to choose — guaranteed, equity, fixed-income, self-directed or insurance — your best and most conservative bet, is a guaranteed plan.

These are the only plans that should be considered by small investors or by people approaching retirement age — say within five years. And they should be the first choice for people who are unwilling to assume the risks that come with holding equity or fixed-income RRSPs, or for those who believe the outlook for stock and bond markets is unfavourable.

As with any other investment, it pays to shop around. Interest rates paid, and registration, administration and withdrawal fees vary widely among institutions.

# chapter six
# *Marriage Contracts*

In an era where one out of four Canadian marriages fails, the well-worn phrase "what is mine, is yours," quickly disintegrates when the time comes to slice up family assets.

Indeed, many couples whose marriages failed after ten, twenty or even thirty years, with thousands of dollars of property involved, have found themselves haggling in lawyer's offices over such mundane matters as who owns the television set and who gets the cat.

Aware of these prospects, many Canadian couples are now taking steps to clearly define their property rights. From teenage newlyweds to skeptical oldtimers heading to the altar for the second or third try, spouses are taking the time to visit lawyers' offices long enough to hammer out the fine points of a marriage contract. Their hope is that by drafting their own document, they will be able to clearly and concisely earmark who owns what, how they intend to share their assets during marriage, and how such assets will be divided up if their marriage fails.

Marriage contracts, of course, are not new. Such contracts have been popular for many years in Quebec where the Civil Code, rather than English common law, determines spousal property rights. What is new is that, under family reform legislation in many provinces, it is possible for couples to draw up a marriage contract that anticipates the disposal of property in the event of marriage breakdown. Until the mid-seventies such contracts were only legal if they did not anticipate or tentatively plan for the eventuality of separation or divorce.

Although the very thought of a marriage contract may be repugnant to those of us who hold traditional views, there are some undeniable facts which should be taken into account in appropriate circumstances. For example, in the undeniable category is the fact that many marriages break up. The splits are seldom neat and clean.

Marriage contracts may be particularly attractive to couples who feel current marital laws either go too far or not far enough in sharing property. Also, people involved in second marriages or common-law relationships might find contracts particularly useful.

If you and your spouse or future spouse are contemplating a marriage contract, and feel that it may provide you with a clearer definition of your property rights, then your first step should be to sit down and openly discuss all joint and individual assets. You should also include in your discussion the extent to which you wish to share these assets and how you would divide your property.

You may wish to design your contract to include:

1. **Full disclosure of assets.** This clause should name all sources of income plus existing assets. Include all real estate and personal property as well as income derived from employment and investments such as stocks and bonds.

2. **Property acquired before marriage.** You may agree that all possessions brought to the marriage will be shared jointly during its course. With a contract you can stipulate that each spouse will retain full ownership of property acquired before marriage even after your vows have been exchanged. (But, keep in mind that in most provinces, you cannot deprive your spouse of the marital home during the course of the marriage, even if you own it. If the marriage breaks down, special rules will likely come into play.)

3. **Property acquired during marriage.** Several options are available here: you may follow provincial reform legislation and agree to share all family assets on a 50-50 basis. Or, you may

draw up a contract which specifically defines that real property acquired during marriage will not be owned on an equal basis but as "tenants in common," that is, in proportion to each person's original investment.

4. Cash and business assets. If this is not covered by law, then you may contract to share (or not share) cash and business holdings. This clause may include registered retirement savings plans, savings accounts, term deposits, stocks, bonds and insurance earnings.

5. Bank accounts. You may want to contract for a joint bank account to keep the day-to-day practicalities of your marriage running smoothly. For instance, you may agree to deposit, in direct proportion to each spouse's income, sufficient funds to pay for such expenditures as the mortgage, food, fuel, cable T.V., telephone, home maintenance, furniture and child care expenses. The balance of your net incomes can then be pooled and divided equally between you for your own use.

6. Child support. While under the law, you cannot opt out of your obligation as a parent, you can contract to limit your obligation. For instance, if one spouse earns less than the other, a clause in your contract could specify that each spouse will pay for a child's maintenance in direct proportion to earnings.

Since it has not been a wide-spread practice for Canadian couples to have marriage contracts, most couples don't know the first thing about them. And many lawyers frankly admit that they have had limited experience in drawing up such documents.

So it's worth examining some pitfalls. Make sure you insert a clause which will allow you to reasonably revise the contract. Otherwise, you may run into difficulties later if you want to modify one clause or change the document completely and your spouse won't co-operate. At this point, you may be forced to stay with what you have.

Make sure, also, that you provide a provision which protects the framework of your contract. Include a clause, for instance, stipulating that even if a particular clause is ruled invalid, the remainder of the contract remains enforceable.

And because people and times change, be sure you include the provision that your documents may be terminated by the written agreement of both you and your spouse.

Once you and your spouse have hammered out what you

wish to contract for, you could legally write your own contract. But it would not be a good idea. Most people have no knowledge of family law and a badly drawn document could create enormous legal problems later. As with wills, the key is to get good legal advice.

A good lawyer, preferably one with experience in family law and specifically in drawing up marriage contracts, will be able to point out areas which you may overlook. A lawyer may also be able to give you some obscure, but beneficial information. For instance, if you live in a jurisdiction where it's not legal to draw up a contract with a separation clause, then it may be possible to adopt the law of another jurisdiction which does have this provision.

Since lawyers usually charge by the hour, you should agree to as much as possible before involving the lawyer. The cost of drawing up a contract doesn't depend on the value of assets involved, but on the time needed to arrive at the finished contract.

Don't settle for legal gobbledygook. Your contract should be written in ordinary layman's language so you can understand it.

Even with the trend in Canadian family law to increased freedom for couples to define their personal property rights, drawing up a marriage contract probably won't hurt. In fact, it may help couples to more clearly define their status with each other and with society.

And with 25% or more of our marriages ending in divorce courts, a contract may be one of the few tangible ways of defining each person's rights and responsibilities in the martrimonial home.

# chapter seven

# *Borrowing Money*

## DO'S AND DON'TS

There aren't too many people who go through life without borrowing money. And, of course, there are pros and cons.

The advantages of borrowing are that we can often use borrowed money to make money, such as for investment purposes; and, it allows us to enjoy things while we earn the money to pay for them, such as buying a home or car.

The disadvantage of borrowing is that it adds considerably to the cost of whatever it is we are borrowing for.

Although there are many guidelines bandied about as to how much a person should or should not borrow, there is really only one that has universal application: don't borrow money that you can't afford to repay when it is due. Even at that, there is a right and wrong way to borrow.

One of the first rules of borrowing is to shop around. A difference of half a percentage can mean a lot of money over the life of a loan.

Most Canadians still have the mistaken impression that all banks, trust companies and other lending institutions are alike, offering the same services at the same rates with the same criteria for granting loans. Yet anyone who shops for a loan quickly discovers that while lenders are similar, rates do differ, as do lending limits and criteria for granting loans. Indeed, these can also vary among branches of the same institution.

It's a recognized fact of banking, for example, just how much managers' discretion varies, as does their willingness to take risks. Go where the bank is hungry. You often have a better chance of getting what you want by going to a new branch in the suburbs than to a bank's main branch.

Even so, your goal is to get an institution to lend you the money you really need. The first step in achieving this is to know what the lending institution will ask for, so you won't be caught off guard.

Be prepared, when walking into any lending institution, to offer specific and detailed information about your income, debts and monthly payments. Of equal importance, you should know the current value of your home, car, insurance, investment portfolio and any other assets. Also prepare an up-to-date list of your liabilities.

Even if you owe a lot of money at the moment, lenders are usually impressed when applicants walk in with a brief personal statement in their hands. This itself will often make the difference in marginal cases.

Any lending institution will want a loan application form filled out either by you or the interviewer. This usually consists of a personal statement listing income, debts and monthly payments, assets and liabilities and employment history. You will also be asked to sign a form giving the lender authority to make inquiries about you to a credit bureau.

Borrowers are often unaware as to how much weight is given stable employment. An employment history of five to ten years with one company often makes the difference — but, obviously not always. A person who switches jobs to gain income, add responsibility, or both, is unlikely to be rejected for this reason. Similarly, a stable residency is a good sign that you're not apt to skip town without paying back a loan.

Lenders also like to know about a spouse's income and generally want the spouse's guarantee.

Many lenders like to discuss a loan with both husband and wife because the wife often sets the family budget. Besides, many creditors believe both parties should acknowledge how loan payments will affect their life styles.

As a rule, bank managers are reluctant to grant loans where repayments may necessitate a cutting back on personal spending because people find it very difficult to change life styles.

Sometimes lenders will require additional security such as bonds or stocks to protect a loan. On personal loans, this security may take the form of a collateral mortgage on a home or, in the case of a loan to buy a car, a chattel mortgage on the vehicle itself.

While your local bank branch is not in the business of lending risk capital for new ventures, such funds are available for the individual who has income from other sources or a net worth which can provide the bank with some security.

Credit unions have been a growing force across the country and in some provinces, especially British Columbia and Quebec, are major competitors of the banks. So, don't overlook this source.

If you have a history of not paying back your debts, or have a habit of switching jobs or residences often for no apparent reason, be prepared to knock on a lot of doors before you get your loan. While lenders want new business, they like to see some stability in your life. As a back-up to the interview, lenders usually obtain a credit report on the applicant.

## THERE'S MORE TO INTEREST THAN JUST THE RATE

When borrowing or lending money (and remember we are really lending money every time we put it in a savings account or term deposit), most people have a tendency to concentrate completely on the interest rate.

There's another factor in the transaction that is just as important, and of which we should never lose sight. It's this: how often is the interest going to be compounded? Or, another way of putting it: how often is the interest going to be calculated and collected, paid or added to the loan, as the case might be?

If you're borrowing money, you want the interest compounded as *infrequently* as possible. Shoot for annual compounding if you can. On the other hand, when you're lending money, you want the interest compounded as *frequently* as possible. Daily, would be great.

Just to illustrate how important the compounding factor is, here are the annual interest figures on a $10,000 loan with interest at 20%. If interest is compounded:

| | |
|---|---|
| annually it's | $2,000 |
| semi-annually it's | $2,100 |
| quarterly it's | $2,155 |
| monthly it's | $2,194 |
| weekly it's | $2,209 |
| daily it would be | $2,213 |

So, if interest is compounded daily, it would be almost 11% higher than if compounded annually. Or, put another way, on a daily compounding you're actually paying 22.13% compared to 20% on an annual basis. Big bucks. Never overlook the compounding period, whichever end of the loan you're on.

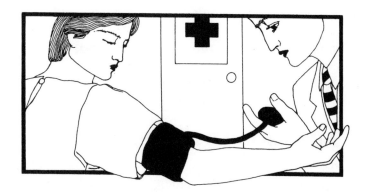

# chapter eight

# *Insurance*

## CHOOSING AN AGENT

The right kind of insurance is one of the best bargains in the world. The trick, of course, is to buy the right kind — and the right amount. This holds true whether we are talking about life insurance, fire insurance, or such esoteric coverage as kidnap insurance. The key to proper insurance coverage is to deal with a reputable, independent agent.

The reasons for dealing with a *reputable* agent are obvious. However, the reasons for dealing with an *independent* agent are not always clearly understood. In order to be able to achieve and sustain his status as an independent agent he must have proven himself as a capable and competent professional, and, even more important to you, the independent agent is not tied to one particular company and can shop the market to obtain the best rate available for coverage appropriate to your particular circumstances.

And that's another thing to bear in mind. It's very rare for any two people to have identical insurance needs. What's right for your neighbor is not necessarily right for you. Your circumstances may be similar, but not likely identical. Again, the best person to advise you is an agent. But bear in mind the agent makes money by selling as much insurance as possible. Your best protection against being ripped off is, as already mentioned, to deal with a reputable, independent agent. How do you find one? Like all other professionals, your best choice is probably the one referred to you by a happy customer.

Now, let's turn attention to some specific types of insurance.

## AUTOMOBILE INSURANCE

Probably the most common mistake in the area of automobile insurance is not having enough. It's a well-known fact that there are people operating automobiles who have no insurance at all.

Public liability insurance — the part of your policy that provides payments to other persons for damages caused by you — is the cheapest component of your automobile insurance policy. In this day and age it doesn't take much of a personal injury accident to run up damages of hundreds of thousands of dollars. When deaths are involved that sum can quickly escalate into a million or more. The potential liability in a multiple-death accident is truly frightening. The lesson is clear. Buy as much public liability insurance as you can.

The other major component of automobile insurance cost is, of course, collision insurance. This is the part of your policy that covers damage to your car. The cost here is dependent on the "deductible amount" — the portion of the repair cost that you agree to pay yourself; say, the first $100, $250, or whatever. A reasonable collision strategy would be to have a fairly low deductible on a new car, increasing as the car gets older and the likelihood of your repairing relatively minor damage diminishes. Indeed, you might even reach a point where you have an old bucket of bolts that you wouldn't bother to repair if it got extensively damaged. In these circumstances you might consider dropping collision coverage altogether.

But, you *never* drop your liability coverage.

Another area to look at is the riders that might be available with your policy. Frequently, very attractive coverage can be tacked on to your insurance policy at very little additional cost covering such risks as medical expenses and theft of personal belongings.

# HOMEOWNERS' INSURANCE

The main point to remember here is that purchasing insurance on your home and its contents is not a one-time, one-shot consideration. Your homeowners' insurance package has to be reviewed *every year*. Even if you are one of the lucky ones who happened to get the right coverage first time around, an automatic renewal each year simply won't do.

Common mistakes, for example, include failing to tell your agent when a valuable extension has been built onto your home, or when some valuable addition — like an expensive painting or a mink coat — has been made to the contents. This could ultimately be a pretty expensive lapse of attention if, upon loss, the agent smiles sympathetically and says, "Sorry, that's not covered."

Here are some key points to discuss with your agent and on which you should be completely clear as to the terms and extent of your coverage:

1. Exactly what risks are covered? You probably should, as a minimum, cover: fire and other accidental causes (such as storms, smoke, etc.) of damage to buildings; fire and theft on contents; public liability and medical expenses (much like your automobile policy); and credit card theft.

2. Be sure to insure for adequate *replacement* cost. Get your agent to determine current replacement cost data for you each year. The automatic inflation increase factor (a percentage per annum in most policies of this type) may not be enough.

3. By the same token, don't insure your land. It won't burn.

4. Determine whether an inventory of contents is required by the insurance company. This is sometimes, but not always, the case. It's a good idea to have one anyway, even if the insurance company doesn't insist on it. If so, don't keep it (or other proof of cost for that matter) where it will burn too if the house and contents go. If an inventory is required, a good way of doing it is to take pictures in each room of its contents. Don't forget to take things out of drawers and closets, and don't forget the camera itself.

5. Always determine what proof of loss will be required under your policy for both buildings and contents.

6. Determine the amount and terms of your coverage when personal items are outside the home — such as in the car or at a hotel while on vacation.

7. What about when you are temporarily away and the house is unoccupied, such as during vacation? Does someone have to check it regularly? Does the water have to be turned off? Be sure to determine what the relevant period of absence is. It will vary in different circumstances.

8. A *vacant* house is different from a temporarily *unoccupied* house. Vacant means no people or furniture. Usually you are only covered for 30 days of vacancy and this might not be enough if, say, you're selling your home and there is a significant period of time between when you move and the new owner takes possession. Extended coverage is available in these circumstances and should be obtained.

9. Are contents covered during a move? Probably not, so specific coverage should be obtained when moving.

10. If you carry on a business in your home it could affect your coverage. Better discuss it with your agent.

11. Be sure your contents coverage is adequate. The automatic "percentage of building coverage" may be inadequate, particularly when applied to specific, valuable items such as works of art, cameras, jewelry, etc. Additional floater policies can bring you up to adequate coverage at relatively little cost.

12. If appraisals of the home or contents are recommended by the agent, be sure the appraiser is reputable. Appraisal reports, like inventories and other valuable proof-of-loss documents, should be kept outside the home, preferably in a safety deposit box.

13. The installation of alarm systems and smoke detectors will likely reduce your premiums — but only if your agent knows you have them.

14. Get your agent to explain "comprehensive" coverage to you. It's the kind you need. As in the case of automobile insurance, check out the floaters and riders available. Once the basic policy is agreed upon there are some truly great bargains available.

15. Use the same agent for all your general insurance (other than life) needs. This will help avoid costly overlaps of coverage.

# CANADA DEPOSIT INSURANCE

You may have an insurance policy that you don't even know about — and you should know about it because it might well affect your choice of savings vehicles. It is the protection provided by the Canada Deposit Insurance Corporation for the benefit of people who have deposits with institutions which are "members."

The Canada Deposit Insurance Corporation (C.D.I.C.) is a Crown Corporation established by a special act of parliament in 1967. Its purpose, as mentioned, is to provide, within clearly defined limits, for the benefit of those who have deposits with member institutions, insurance against the loss of such deposits because of the insolvency of a member institution.

Membership in the C.D.I.C. is restricted to banks, trust companies and mortgage loan companies. Any such institution which is incorporated under federal law *must* be a member. Provincially incorporated institutions become members only after making a formal application which in turn will be accepted by the C.D.I.C. only if the government of the province concerned has approved the application and if prescribed standards and conditions are met.

If you don't know that you're dealing with a federally incorporated institution, there are really only three ways to determine whether the institution you're dealing with is a member. It might be displaying an official membership sign; you can ask at the institution itself; or, the only sure way to find out, you can enquire of the C.D.I.C. itself. It's located in Ottawa and can be reached by asking at the federal government.

The C.D.I.C. insures savings and chequing accounts, money orders, deposit receipts, guaranteed investment certificates, debentures and other obligations issued by member institutions.

The maximum amount of deposit insurance in force is, at the time of writing, $60,000 for each *person*, i.e. depositor, and that limit applies to the combined total of principal and interest. It should be noted, though, that to be insurable, a term deposit must be redeemable no later than five years after the date of deposit.

The maximum amount applies to the combined total of all separate deposit accounts any one person has at the same institution. This includes the combined total of all deposits in all branches of the same institution. You can only increase your coverage by spreading your business among various institutions. Spreading it among different branches of the same institution doesn't work. Simply stated, a person's deposits are separately insured to the maximum in each institution which is a member of the Corporation. However, joint deposits are insured separately from deposits in the individual names of the parties to the joint deposit. The joint deposit is essentially looked upon as a separate person for this purpose.

An area of great confusion in the context of deposit insurance is whether it applies to registered retirement savings plans and registered home ownership savings plans with member institutions.

The short answer is that it does not apply. But, like almost everything else these days such a straight answer doesn't tell the whole story. So, let's try to unravel the mystery a bit.

Neither an RHOSP nor an RRSP is itself covered by deposit insurance. Neither are the contributions made to such plans covered *per se*. But, remember that when you make a contribution to such a plan you are really handing over your money to a trustee who invests it on your behalf. Now that trustee, in the capacity of acting on your behalf, is a separate *person* insofar as deposit insurance is concerned. Accordingly, if the institution invests the contribution in a type of deposit qualifying for deposit insurance — such as term deposits not exceeding five years — the protection, up to the maximum per trustee per institution, is available.

Remember, though, that in these circumstances it is the trustee which is insured and not the holder of the plan. If the Canada Deposit Insurance Corporation was called upon to meet the obligations of the member institution, the Corporation would pay the trustee, not the contributor. The contributor would then have to look to the trustee for reimbursement.

This raises the question of what the deposit insurance coverage is on a trust deposit made by a trustee acting for several beneficiaries. If the member institution is notified of the separate interest of each beneficiary in the deposits, then the interests of each beneficiary would be separately insured to the maximum.

This raises another important point. If you are the executor, administrator or trustee of an estate with two or more beneficiaries, the maximum insurance applies to the entire estate unless you notify the member institution of the interest of each beneficiary. If you do so, each beneficiary will be insured up to the maximum.

As is usually the case, things are slightly different in Quebec, but there is really no different effect on the depositors.

Deposits with federally incorporated companies are insured by the Canada Deposit Insurance Corporation regardless of where the deposits are located. Quebec has its own deposit insurance plan (the Quebec Deposit Insurance Board). Under the terms of an agreement between the C.D.I.C. and the Q.D.I.B., deposits made in Quebec with provincially incorporated companies are guaranteed by the Q.D.I.B., while deposits made outside Quebec with such companies are guaranteed by the C.D.I.C.

Always remember that the C.D.I.C. insures against a loss arising only from the insolvency of a member institution. Other losses, such as theft, are not covered.

## LIFE INSURANCE

Canadians spend billions of dollars on life insurance premiums each year, but many have no idea of what product to buy, who to buy it from, or how much to pay for it.

When buying a new car, it seems natural for most of us to spend days poring over brochures, visiting showrooms, testing models and checking with friends. But when it comes to buying life insurance — a product that is more important and often more costly than a car — most Canadians can't tell a lemon from a plum.

Unfortunately, only their survivors will know for sure.

Canadians already are the most heavily insured people, on a *per capita* basis, in the world.

Despite this almost morbid, though necessary, pre-occupation with preparing for death, many Canadians are under-insured, pay too much for their life insurance, and often buy the wrong kinds of coverage.

Who's to blame? Well, just about everybody. Individuals, for being so careless about a product that will cost many thousands of dollars over the years. Society, for being so nervous about dealing with death. Even though we pay a lot of money for protection, most us don't like to think about premature death and the hardship it might place on our survivors. The life insurance industry, for not doing enough to make things easier for consumers. The industry surrounds itself with a confusing array of actuarial technicalities, needlessly complex terminology and mind-bending numbers. As a result, most life insurance buyers end up bewildered.

You can save anywhere from a few dollars to a few thousand dollars on life insurance if you follow a couple of basic rules:

1. Ask questions and compare prices. That may seem difficult — there are hundreds of organizations selling life insurance in Canada, and each uses its own particular names for various kinds of coverage. But guides are available and it is not necessary to check the pricing structure of every company. Some comparison is worthwhile, though, because prices for the same product often vary widely.
2. Make sure you know what you want to buy — in other words, what you want to protect. This is the most difficult, but most crucial, aspect of buying life insurance.

Most people buy life insurance to replace a source of income that would be eliminated by a death.

For example, a thirty-year-old man with a mortgage, car loan and two young children usually takes care of his obligations with a monthly pay cheque. If he dies, his family will still need a pay cheque of some sort to pay the bills.

Each individual has different needs, but generally a wage earner without substantial assets and with dependents should consider buying life insurance equal to about ten or twelve times his or her annual salary.

The amount can vary, depending on how old you are (the younger you are, if you have dependents, generally the more insurance you need), what other assets you have and how many dependents you are supporting.

If you buy $200,000 of insurance, it would yield, at 10% interest, income of $20,000 a year for your survivors. But over the years inflation could take a sizeable bite out of the buying power of that money, and your survivors may be forced to draw on capital to maintain a reasonable standard of living.

Undoubtedly, a CLU (chartered life underwriter) is most knowledgeable about life insurance matters. If the agent you are dealing with is not a CLU, it would be wise to seek a second opinion from a CLU. Many people also feel it is a good idea to double check *any* agent's recommendations (CLU or not) with an independent consultant, such as an accountant, lawyer, banker or other knowledgeable person you trust. Indeed, until such time as you have found an independent life agent (one who is not forced to sell a particular company's product, but is free to make the best deal for you — which could be the case even if he works out of the one company's office or branch) whose advice you trust completely, the second opinion route is a sensible one. However, when going this route, you, the agent and your third party consultant should always meet *together* before a final decision is made. This will save you a lot of time in that any disagreements can be thrashed out by your two advisors directly without the necessity of you having to ferry arguments pro and con between them. But always remember, the agent is the most knowledgeable about insurance matters.

It isn't that the insurance industry can't be trusted — it can. The problem is that agents are human and some of them occasionally try to sell a product that meets their commission requirements more than it meets your insurance needs. But, as mentioned, an experienced, independent life agent with a solid reputation in the community knows more about life insurance than any accountant, lawyer or bank manager. So, you have a tightrope to walk. The pack suggested in the preceding paragraph is probably your best bet. See page 66 for some tips on dealing with an insurance agent. It will help you deal with the problem if you understand it better.

## WHOLE LIFE VS TERM

There are two basic types of life insurance, both good products, but each set up to meet entirely different needs: "whole life" and "term." For most people, term is the one to buy.

Term insurance is cheaper because it provides protection for age groups in which the mortality rate is low. Even at age 60, relatively few policyholders die. Hence, yearly premiums tend to be low. Term premiums are generally much lower than whole life premiums for young people.

While term insurance provides temporary protection, say, for one year, five years, or until a specified age, whole life provides protection for the whole of your life. Premiums are higher because the risk is greater that the insurance company will have to pay a death benefit. If fact, they *will* have to pay unless the policy lapses or is cancelled.

Whole life insurance can be useful for those who have taxable estates, business partners, special care problems (such as a handicapped heir), the possibility of a temporary period during which one might not be able to pay premiums, a real reason to believe that one might someday be uninsurable, or if insurance will *always* be needed.

But too many people end up with costly whole life products because they don't know any better. And the life insurance companies are not about to discourage that flow of extra premiums — especially since many whole life policies never pay a death benefit. They often lapse or are surrendered before the policyholder dies, for example, by policyholders who discover that their policies don't suit their needs, or that they can't afford them.

Many people don't need insurance in their old age and shouldn't pay for it. Most people plan to retire by age 65 and expect to be financially self-sufficient by then. If they are not, life insurance premiums at that age might only add to the drain on their incomes.

If you're pretty sure you'll not need insurance when you're old and gray, why try to pay off steep whole life premiums when you're young?

This is not to say whole life is a bad product. It isn't. But its uses are limited and you should get to know them before you sign on the dotted line.

A final word of caution: beware of life agents who try to sell whole life policies on the grounds that they are good vehicles for saving.

In fact, whole life insurance does not provide for any savings, although the cash values that come with these policies may sometimes seem like savings.

The cash value of a whole life policy belongs to the life insurance company, not the policyholder. If you want to take part of your "savings" out, the life insurance company will charge interest on what they call a "loan." At the same time the amount of your insurance coverage will be reduced by the amount of the "loan" with no reduction in the amount of your premium.

But, this raises an interesting point. If you have a whole life policy with a cash surrender value (the term given the so-called "savings" portion) it is probable that you can "borrow" against it at a very reasonable interest rate. You might be able to make money by simply borrowing the maximum amount you can and putting the proceeds into term deposits. But, check it carefully before doing so. And remember that your "loan" reduces your insurance coverage.

Now let's turn attention to situations where whole life insurance might be appropriate.

It's often been said there are two things of which we can be certain — death and taxes. Whole life insurance, however, can make the latter easier for your dependents or business partners when the former happens.

This applies to relatively few Canadians (most do not have taxable estates or business partners) — but if you do, or if you fall into one of the other categories explained earlier, take a close look at whole life insurance.

The main reason for buying whole life is to create ready cash at death. The cash can be used to pay taxes arising on death (such as on deemed capital gains), or to look after funeral and burial expenses, or in the case of a business, to provide funds to ease what could be a bumpy transition when a key executive dies. Term insurance doesn't serve this need because it becomes prohibitively expensive — and ultimately impossible to buy — as you grow older.

But for most people, this is academic, because they won't need the ready cash that whole life will provide in old age, and they shouldn't pay for it.

Most of us do not have to worry about death taxes. As for funeral expenses, many Canadians can provide for that out of a small savings fund. Otherwise, a small $5,000 to $10,000 whole life policy might be worthwhile.

An important application for whole life insurance is in business. Business partners, for example, can insure each other for a large sum, so that if one dies, the other will have the funds to buy the deceased partner's share of the business, pay large company debts and survive the first year.

For example, if one partner needed to borrow to pay for a deceased partner's share of the business, that loan could cost most of a company's pre-tax earnings, whereas a single premium whole-life policy might only cost a fraction of that amount. Life insurance meets the need.

Even after you've decided which is the most appropriate form of life coverage — term or whole life; and for the vast majority of people it should be term — you will still have to decide from among a number of alternatives with wonderful sounding names. Examples are single premium plans, joint and last survivor plans, level premium plans, reducing term plans, convertible plans, and on and on.

Books could be written about these various options. Space will only allow me to advise you to be absolutely sure you understand exactly what you're buying. The best way to achieve that is to deal firmly, objectively, and appropriately with the agent.

When you have determined the amount and type of life insurance coverage you need, a good place to start is to obtain as much group term coverage as is available to you. This is usually the cheapest form of life insurance coverage you can find. Most employers provide group life plans, and you are often able to obtain more than the minimum coverage provided by paying a low additional premium. Ask about it.

Also, if you're a member of a professional organization, a fraternity club, or a union, they often provide very cheap group term coverage. Ask about that, too.

## DEALING WITH A LIFE AGENT

What can you do to protect yourself when dealing with life insurance agents? The odds are you will be dealing with a competent, sincere agent, but unless you have a thorough and detailed knowledge of the business — or the agent personally — you can't be sure.

The agent will know more about life insurance than you. At the very least he or she will have a finely honed sales pitch, and you won't have the ammunition to argue.

But there are a few simple things you can do.

1. Insist that the agent keep things simple. Don't be ashamed of your lack of knowledge. Ask any and all questions, even if they seem silly.
2. Talk to more than one agent. Invite two or three to your home and make sure at least one favours term insurance. In this way you get more than one side of a life insurance argument (and there are many sides).
3. Talk to each agent about what the others have proposed. There are two main things to consider — cost and benefit.

**4.** Finally, phone a few other companies to get price quotations on the policy and amounts of coverage you think are best suited to your needs. In this way you foster competition among life agents and their companies, and you will at least have some choice.

# DISABILITY INSURANCE

For most young breadwinners, the odds are greater they will become disabled before age 65 than that they will die. Yet, many people who wouldn't for a moment not have life insurance will go merrily along every day with no disability coverage whatsoever.

You should be sure that you have some form of disability insurance to cover the situation of your being unable to work. Many employers provide group disability coverage, and many professional organizations and unions also provide such plans. Fraternity organizations or service clubs often provide group coverage as well. And, of course, commercial insurance companies have disability plans available.

The technicalities of disability insurance are even more confusing than life insurance rules. So, here are a few things to keep in mind when buying such coverage:

**1.** As always, deal only with a reputable agent and company.

**2.** Make sure you understand each and every provision of your coverage. For example, to collect would you have to be *totally* disabled, or would disability to carry on your *normal* vocation qualify you?

**3.** If you have more than one form of coverage, e.g. a group plan at work and a private or professional organization plan as well, be sure that one doesn't cancel out the other. If they do, you're paying one set of premiums with no hope of getting anything in return.

The main thing to remember, of course, is if you don't have disability coverage, you may be subjecting your dependents to as much risk as if you didn't have life insurance.

# chapter nine
## *Swiss Banks*

The very mention of Swiss banks conjures up visions of Mafia, drug money, the jet set and high rollers. Very little truth about Swiss banks is disclosed in such stories.

Yet there are some truths in the myths. Swiss banks have built a reputation for financial freedom, privacy and stability. The Swiss have enjoyed monetary freedom unparalleled in any other country of the world. When economic conditions deteriorate world wide, governments tend to impose regulations such as foreign currency restrictions, wage and price controls, and gold ownership bans. The Swiss tend to avoid such over-regulation.

The political and economic stability of Switzerland, demonstrated by its neutrality in world wars and the absence of unexpected government regulation, has given Swiss bankers the opportunity to build a reputation based on reliability, competence and efficiency.

Customers of Swiss banks can rest assured that their business dealings with the bank will remain confidential, except for situations which will be discussed later. The concept of secrecy was entrenched in the banking laws of Switzerland as far back as 1934, and revised and reaffirmed as recently as 1971. The laws apply to the banks and their officers and employees. Anyone divulging information obtained in his capacity as an officer or employee of a bank could be punished by a prison term or a hefty fine. Implementation of these measures is largely the result of bribery, blackmail and other devious means used by the Gestapo during the Nazi regime to obtain information about German citizens' foreign holdings.

The duty of secrecy ends, however, when a higher public interest clashes with the bank's client's personal interest in the preservation of anonymity. Criminal activities of account holders are not protected by banking secrecy legislation. In cases of arson, bankruptcy, blackmail, tax fraud, falsification of documents, common and organized crime, murder, narcotics trading and dealing in firearms, following the judgment of a Swiss Court, banks will disclose information to entitled authorities. However, in cases of political, military, exchange control or tax evasion offences punishable in other countries, Switzerland declines legal co-operation.

In recent years Swiss secrecy laws have received a great deal of media coverage as a result of severe criticism aimed at this banking tradition by other countries, and primarily the United States. Switzerland has signed several treaties with other countries to provide legal assistance in prosecuting criminal cases where the crime would be a crime under Swiss law. In cases of tax evasion in Canada and the U.S., which is a failure to declare or pay taxes and considered a crime in these countries, revenue authorities have been unable to gain access to information in Swiss Bank accounts of the suspects because simple tax evasion is not considered a crime in Switzerland, therefore, no disclosure; hence the stories of abetting crime. Switzerland expects its laws to be respected, just as it makes no attempt to apply its laws elsewhere.

With its reputation for freedom, privacy and the stability of its political system and currency, Switzerland has had a significant inflow of capital from investors around the world. The diverse services provided by Swiss banks include commercial banking, portfolio management, mortgages, capital market financing and custodial services. The most highly publicized aspect of Swiss banking, the Swiss numbered account, is the Swiss banking practice that is most misunderstood. Let's clear up some of the misconceptions about the functioning of this type of account.

What's so special about a Swiss numbered account? All bank accounts have numbers. The difference is that the identity of the holder of the Swiss account is not shown on the account card itself and it would be known to only a few top officials in the bank. All instructions for transactions are made by using only the number of the account.

Here's how you open a Swiss numbered account. First, the account usually must be opened in person, and depending on the bank selected this could necessitate a trip to Switzerland. Tough penalty to pay. However, a few of the big Swiss banks have opened branch offices in Toronto and Montreal and as a result it could probably be opened here. The bank manager would likely require a reference letter, information about your business, your assets and your family situation. A signature card, being your coded "signature," is kept on file. If any other family members are authorized to use the account, their coded signatures would also be kept on file. The coded signature is the famous number, which could be either a pure number or a code word and number.

Most of the banks do not specify minimum balances, but might refuse to open an account for a small amount. People have been known to open an account with a couple of hundred dollars, but a few thousand would be more desirable. The reason for some banks refusing to open small accounts is the administrative cost and paper-work involved. Service charges are minimal.

Subject to the bank's acceptance of you as a customer you now have a numbered account. Should you desire, it could consist of sub-accounts for foreign currencies and securities, precious metals and art custodial services. Written orders affecting any of these accounts must bear your coded signature. They are never signed with actual names. Transactions may be made by written instruction, telephone or in person. In the latter case the transaction would take place in a private room with only the manager or other top officials of the bank present. Under Swiss law full signature names must appear on a cheque. If you wish to preserve your anonymity, a bank will issue a cheque for you for a very nominal fee.

There are several advantages to a numbered account. First, the central location of Switzerland within Europe affords easy communication with other industrialized nations. Switzerland's neutrality during the world wars and years of uninterrupted peace have contributed to economic stability and development. When making an investment these are important factors to consider and this advantage has resulted in a significant inflow of capital into Switzerland as economic, political and social conditions worsen in other countries. Historically, the Swiss have permitted currency freedom to residents and non-residents which enables anyone to convert his currency to any other. However, some restrictive rules were adopted in 1975 and 1976 with respect to the investment by non-residents in Swiss currency.

Also the free ownership of gold and other metals is allowed. This contributes to the attraction of the numbered account since transfers of an endangered currency to Swiss francs protects the asset value, and the anonymity of the numbered account provides security.

The numbered account also affords freedom from persecution. For example, in countries where foreign exchange restrictions exist, an individual can successfully transfer funds to a numbered account without leaving a trace. When the individual and his or her assets are out of the country of residence, the assets can be disposed of without any risk. To avoid the government of the country of residence gaining any knowledge of such an account, you can request that all correspondence be held at the bank.

In South American, Eastern European and Middle Eastern countries the nationalization of mines, oil wells and factories has left many disgruntled owners without rewards for their past efforts. In the face of a threat of nationalization, the earnings of foreign participants could be transferred to numbered accounts to avoid loss when nationalization takes place.

The banking secrecy laws furnish protection and confidentiality to holders of accounts. Many people in the public eye, such as politicians, entertainers and movie stars, enjoy the anonymity of the numbered account and hold them for that reason. *All* Swiss accounts are subject to the secrecy laws and it is this additional feature of numbered accounts that is considered a necessity for many individuals. The pros of holding a numbered account are obvious for individuals in certain circumstances such as outlined above, but the cons must be considered prior to making a decision.

Some of the disadvantages are strictly psychological. Many of us feel a sense of security in keeping our investments close to home and feel a certain discomfort about having holdings many thousands of miles away, despite Switzerland's strong track record. Numbered accounts offend legality and morality in many countries of the world, and there is that apprehension about the trouble ahead if the authorities discover it.

For Canadian and U.S. residents it is not illegal to hold numbered accounts. However, in the case of the U.S., there is a requirement that all foreign holdings be disclosed on your annual tax return. As long as the account produces no income, there can be no tax evasion. In Canada, a tax is levied on the world income of residents and if there were interest or dividends in the account, this fact would have to be reported. In addition, when accounts holding foreign currencies are closed and the funds repatriated, any appreciation of the foreign currency relative to the Canadian dollar might be subject to tax.

Getting back to the U.S. for a moment — even though the penalties for non-disclosure of foreign holdings may not be severe, there is the loss of anonymity upon discovery by the authorities. Weighing the benefits of privacy and the potential consequences of being found out allows each individual to make a decision that he or she can live with.

The transfer of funds to a Swiss account without leaving a trace presents an obstacle. Records of all cheques cashed are kept by Canadian banks on microfilm. However, small amounts could be transferred by money orders, which do not require the sender's signature, and several of these could be sent at one time. The use of cashier's cheques is also a possibility. Of course, you can always stuff a black bag with cash and take a trip.

In countries which impose foreign currency controls, transferring assets can be a costly procedure. First it is necessary to buy hard currency illegally in the black market of the resident country. A stiff premium will be paid for the currency depending on the size of the transaction and the conditions of the local and international currency. A commission is also levied by the broker who arranges the transfer of the funds.

The question of Swiss taxes also arises. On Swiss deposits and securities bearing interest or earning dividends held by non-residents a withholding tax is levied and withheld by the banks when the income is deposited to the account. At present there is a tax convention between Canada and Switzerland which eases the tax burden.

As mentioned, Switzerland occasionally imposes restrictions limiting the inflow of foreign funds. You should always keep abreast of the current situation.

Now that the pros and cons of the numbered account have been considered, the decision is yours. It may make no economic sense, but the snob appeal is irresistible to many.

# chapter ten

# *Lottery Wins*

This chapter is not for rich folks who are accustomed to handling vast sums of money. We're going to make some suggestions as to what you should do if you hit it lucky in one of the lotteries. Of course, no general answer exists which could be appropriately applied in all circumstances, and it is obvious that for some people a lottery win wouldn't change their lives a great deal. But, here's what winners should logically do.

First the biggy — if your number comes up for the million dollar prize. What you do that night and the morning after might set the course for the rest of your life. So stop and think about it.

The first thing you must do is suppress the urge to go out in the street and announce your good fortune to the world. The next thing to do, even if you are in Tobermory, Charlottetown or Moose Jaw, is hop on the first plane to the lottery head office to be there when it opens in the morning. That million dollars could earn a few hundred dollars interest per day — so any delay in picking up the prize means money lost.

But you've got more to worry about than just money in a million-dollar situation. You may not be able to escape the publicity since the lotteries almost always insist that you agree to have your name publicized in the case of really big wins. This means that a horde of full-time money chasers, including less fortunate relatives and friends, will learn of your good fortune. You will be flooded with requests for money — not only will beggars and crackpots be after you, but so will charities, salesmen, advisors, investment counsellors and hopeful entrepreneurs with plans for a better mousetrap. Don't forget extortionists. People have been kidnapped for sums much smaller than a million.

The next person you have to be wary of is yourself. Resist those urges to go out and buy fancy cars and flashy jewellery. In fact, don't make any rash decisions. After cashing in the ticket and getting the money earning interest for you, pay off all your debts, particularly your mortgage. Then, put all the money, except for $10,000, into a three-month guaranteed term deposit with your bank. Follow this so far? Now, take your $10,000, your family and your suntan oil and disappear to an undisclosed haven and have a holiday for a month or so.

Why disappear? To escape the storm of publicity with its temptations and possible dangers, and to take time to adjust to your sudden wealth. Your money is locked into an account you can't touch — and the interest that accumulates will more than pay for your vacation. After the initial euphoria wears off, you'll be in a much better position to decide exactly what to do with the money — what to buy, how to invest, how much to give away. You will certainly need professional help in the conduct of your financial affairs. Get yourself the best advice you can from a reputable professional.

By far the most important thing to remember is not to go off the deep end that first night or next morning. A million will certainly change your life — but you want it to change in ways and at a pace that you can control.

Another thing not to do is to immediately begin living like the millionaires. If you move to their part of town, and try to move in their circles, you're apt to find your life-long friends (not to mention relatives) don't relate to you any more, and your new colleagues may not accept you either. Make your changes in life style slowly and carefully.

Now, what about winning $100,000? Well, $100,000 is a nice manageable amount of money. It won't fulfill your wildest dreams of wealth and luxury, but it can satisfy your immediate cash needs and bring you a measure of comfort and security. There are a few things you should do and some you should emphatically not do with your hundred grand.

Don't immediately quit your job. $100,000 is simply not enough to retire on, unless you're close to retirement age anyway and have lots of other security. The annual income from perfectly safe investments would be far less than you can live on comfortably.

Don't sell your $60,000 house, add the $100,000 to what you receive and put it all down on a $160,000 house uptown. You will still have your mortgage and other debts, and you may find that the taxes and other expenses of the larger home are more than you can handle.

One hundred thousand is enough, let's say, to give you a nice head start in life, but not enough to change your whole life style — not enough to run wild on for any length of time.

Now, here's what you *should* do. First, collect the money immediately and get it into the bank earning interest. Then pay off all your debts, particularly your mortgage — this itself will put you a good 15 to 20 years ahead of your less fortunate friends and neighbors. You could, perhaps, leave the cash in the bank for five years or so, almost doubling it, but your interest would be taxable while your mortgage interest, at a higher rate, is probably non-deductible, which means your real interest cost may be almost double the rate you think it is. You're better off to eliminate mortgage interest from your life altogether, especially since your home will continue to increase in value.

Then, but only then, you can buy a few things you need, or want, such as a new car, furniture, a cottage, or an extraordinary vacation.

An alternative that many people might consider is this. If you already own your home, or don't wish to own one at all, use the $100,000 to improve your life. If you're stuck in a job you don't like, or if there's something you've always wanted to do, such as get a degree, learn a trade or write novels, your windfall gives you a golden opportunity to give it a try. By living off the interest and consuming the principal reasonably carefully, you could buy yourself at least three, and maybe more, years of freedom to pursue your personal ambition — and this is a chance, let's face it, that very few people ever get.

The most important thing, however, is not to go head-over-heels off the deep end with a $100,000 lottery win. Don't quit your job right away and don't speculate with the money. Pay off all your debts — the most vital key to financial prosperity in the long run — have a little fun, treat yourself a bit, then wisely invest whatever is left, perhaps in guaranteed investment certificates, Canada Savings Bonds and other forms of safe securities.

# chapter eleven

# *Investing in Real Estate*

There are a number of different ways to invest in real estate: owning your own home; owning a recreation property; owning property which you rent to others; owning raw land; owning shares in real estate corporations; and, investing in mortgages. The first two mentioned — owning your own home or a recreation property — are probably the most common, and certainly the largest, investments that people make. Ironically, though, many people don't look upon them as investments, but rather concentrate on their usefulness as filling a need or fulfilling a wish. At the same time, they represent the investment vehicle with which most individuals are most familiar. Nevertheless, some points in connection therewith are not well understood. And, there are misconceptions.

This chapter will remind you of some things you've forgotten about real estate as an investment, clarify some others, and perhaps bring out some considerations that you hadn't thought about at all.

## YOUR BEST INVESTMENT

Your residence is probably the best investment you will ever make.

Although not a perfect hedge against inflation — but, then, nothing is — over the long-term, residential real estate probably comes closest. Couple this with the fact that there is no capital gains tax payable on any increase in value throughout the period during which it qualifies as your principal residence, and you will see it is very difficult to find a better long-term investment.

In addition, there is no other investment that carries with it such utilitarian value. We all need four walls around us, a roof over our heads, and a place to go to the bathroom.

Furthermore, there is probably no other investment that consistently contributes so much to our everyday enjoyment. And with the coming of the age of home computers, video games, pay television and the like, this trend is apt to increase.

The lesson is clear. If you can afford to buy — don't rent. Even if you have to settle for less attractive accommodation, or a less desirable area, you are far better off being an owner than sitting on the outside looking in while property values continue to get away from you.

Even though most people buy their homes (particularly their first one) based on what they can afford, there are a number of things to keep in mind. For example, the price of the home itself is only one of the components of its total cost to you. The interest cost of financing it has to be taken into consideration. Furthermore, you're going to have to be directly responsible for a number of additional costs which were previously built right into your rent, such as repairs, insurance, property taxes, and water; and in some cases electricity and heating.

There are also one-time costs involved in buying a house which have to be taken care of. These include legal fees, moving, land transfer taxes in some jurisdictions, and other so-called "closing adjustments" such as oil in the tank and property taxes already paid by the vendor for the period of time during the current year in which you will be the owner.

It's rare to find a house that you can just move into. Usually you'll have to do some decorating and repairing and you'll often need some additional drapes, curtains, furniture and tools. For example, if you live in an apartment you aren't likely to own a lawnmower, rake and snow shovel.

All these costs have to be considered.

Another consideration is what type of a house you want — an

old one or a new one? Here are a couple of points to keep in mind when making this decision. With an older house you are usually in a position to negotiate things like, drapes, fixtures and appliances. If you like the idea of having a new house remember that you are really starting from scratch. A new house usually has absolutely nothing in it — no appliances, carpets, fixtures or drapes. These items are very costly if you have to go out and buy them new.

Now, how do you find your house? The two most popular routes to follow when looking for a house are registering with a real estate agency and having them look for you, or looking in the newspaper yourself.

If you register with a real estate agency, you simply tell the agent how much you can afford to pay and the area in which you want to live. The agent will then call you when something comes available. This doesn't cost you anything.

Right about now is the time to get an "Interest Amortization Tables" book. You'll find this to be the most helpful thing to have handy when you're looking at homes. This book tells you how much your mortgage payments will be each month at whatever percent of interest you'll be paying over the amortization period you choose.

This book is quite simple to get. Most bookstores will have one, and if they don't carry it on the shelf, will order it for you.

When the agent takes you to look at homes, don't be afraid to look in cupboards and closets. If the people who are selling the home are there, ask them questions, like, how much are the heating bills each month? Is the house insulated? How long have you lived there? What kind of public transit is available? When you find a house you are really interested in, go back and see it again before you make an offer.

After you've seen the house at least twice and you know you can afford the monthly bills and the mortgage payment, make an offer to purchase.

Have the agent write-up a formal offer. Make sure you *list* everything you want left in the house, like fixtures, broadloom, stove, refrigerator, washer and dryer — don't just say appliances. You may want to put clauses in your offer such as, "this home has never been insulated with urea-formaldehyde." Another clause might be that the people who now own the house must take *every-thing* with them when they move out other than what you have listed in the offer. You don't want to move in and find they have left all the old furniture and garbage they didn't think was worth taking with them to *their* new home.

Now that you have your offer ready, no matter what the agent says, *don't sign anything!* See a lawyer. An offer to purchase is a binding, legal document that should be carefully reviewed by a lawyer familiar with real estate matters. It is also important that you see a lawyer of your choice. Don't use the same lawyer as the vendor or the real estate agent. A little time and money now could save a fortune in dollars and disappointment later on.

Another thing to keep in mind when planning to purchase a home is that the federal and provincial governments have in recent years introduced many and varied plans to assist homebuyers, particularly first-time buyers. A good example is the Registered Home Ownership Savings Plan. Also, from time to time both levels of government have introduced temporary purchase assistance grants. Because these plans come and go and are changed with almost every federal and provincial budget, it could be misleading to get into any details of them here. But, if you're contemplating the purchase of a home, especially if you're a first-time buyer, you should enquire as to what government assistance or income tax breaks might be available. Your accountant, lawyer, bank or trust company manager should be able to advise you.

Also, many of the comments under the heading of "Buying a Country Property" apply as well to your regular residence, so read on.

## RECREATION PROPERTIES

Perhaps you should consider buying a cottage, farm, chalet or other recreation property as protection against the ravages of inflation.

We usually think of such properties in terms of family vacations or a country retreat where we can enjoy the outdoor life. All well-located recreation properties offer these benefits, of course, but they might also be a smart investment.

An example is in order. Say you have $35,000 which you plan to invest, re-investing the income each year to create a retirement nest egg. The first thing you must take into consideration is that the income will be taxable — and for many people this means they will lose between 40 to 50 percent of their earnings.

Say you invest at 10 percent. Your money would earn $3,500 in the first year — but, at a 50 percent tax rate, you would pay $1,750 in income tax. Your investment would total $36,750. After five years you would have about $45,000.

Seems okay, doesn't it? Well it's not — because inflation will likely have eroded the value of your money substantially. In recent years inflation has averaged over 10 percent in Canada. If we apply a 10 percent inflation loss each year for five years to that $45,000 it turns out that that amount of money would be worth only about $25,000.

Your nest egg is shrinking fast.

Now, let's say that instead of salting your $35,000 away for a rainy day, you bought a lakeside cottage. It is a fair assumption that the value of the cottage and lot will appreciate over a period of time. At the very least, you can safely assume that over the long-term your cottage will stay even with inflation.

Five years from now — if we take the same 10 percent annual inflation rate — the cottage would be worth at least $56,000. This is simply the equivalent, in these inflated dollars, of your $35,000 in current money.

You would, however, have paid expenses on the cottage — property taxes, hydro, maintenance, etc., which we can estimate to be $700. If we apply a 10 percent inflation rate to this, you would pay about $1,000 in expenses in five years time — or a total of about $4,200 over the five years. Take that from the inflated value of the cottage, and you can only be certain of $51,800.

But consider the intangibles.

First, we can assume that over the years you and your family will enhance the value of the cottage through your own efforts. Clearing the land, improving the waterfront, putting in flower beds, shrubbery, etc., are all chores you and your family will want to do anyway — and these improvements will add substantially to resale value.

Second, you may contribute much of your own labour to improvements to the building itself — redecorating, constructing built-in furniture, perhaps putting on an addition or even building a guest cottage. You will get far more than just your money back when you sell.

Third, you will not find it difficult to rent your cottage during periods when you aren't using it, to help offset costs.

Fourth, you will save on family vacation costs every year you use your own cottage.

Fifth, and most important, desirable real estate in highly popular markets has traditionally increased in value more rapidly over the long-term than general inflation. Population pressures plus the relative scarcity of good vacation land will help push up the resale value of your cottage over the years. Just be certain you choose well — waterfront access on a popular body of water, no more than three or four hours drive from a major population center.

Of course no one can predict the future, so you will never be absolutely certain that any financial decision you make today will turn out to be the very best for you five years from now. If inflation were to fall off drastically, for example, things could turn out quite differently — but not likely.

An informed guess, based on past experience, is that you could enjoy all the pleasure of cottage ownership and create a retirement nest egg at the same time.

## BUYING A COUNTRY PROPERTY

An old home, fresh air, a garden, peace and quiet, the promise of easy living away from the stress of the city, all send people scurrying into the countryside in search of dreamland. Actually finding your paradise, or knowing it when you see it, is quite another matter.

Locating a country home is not at all like buying one in town. Business in Ruralsville is conducted at a more leisurely and far less exacting pace.

If you're heading in that direction, here are some suggestions that might make life a little easier for you:

1. Choose an area that interests you and then spend a fair amount of time getting to know it well. Drive around the roads, call into the stores and service stations and get the owner talking about properties that might be for sale if and when there is a buyer. Watch the local papers and visit properties that are up for sale. Have local real estate brokers show you everything that even vaguely meets your desires. There is no better way to learn about what you like and don't like.

2. Read about old homes, particularly articles that list problems you might encounter and what it's apt to cost you to set them

right. It is useful to know, for example, that a beat-up looking building with a solid foundation may have more life left in it than a beautifully painted ranch style with a leaky basement.

3. Be skeptical about anything good you are told about a property and remember that if any faults are mentioned, you can bet they will be humdingers.

4. Ask embarrassing questions like: "It's impossible to heat the upstairs in February, isn't it?"

5. Never buy a country home in the summer. Look, certainly; probe, by all means; show you are interested if you must; but, *don't* make an offer. October, or even better, a rainy day in November, is the best time to talk money. The country looks good enough during the summer to blind you. Vendors and agents know that and adjust their prices accordingly. In late fall, on the other hand, your July manor may more closely resemble the house from the movie *Psycho*.

6. Avoid like the plague being enthralled by one aspect of the property. The pond at the bottom of the hill won't keep you warm in January. An old barn can be better enjoyed in a painting on the wall than through a drafty window. Owning a home "well back from the road" is privacy in the summer but a curse in the winter and spring.

7. Check the land. Walk it with the broker or vendor and determine roughly where the boundaries are. Walking it is also the best way to find the swamp. Find out if anyone has access rights across the property.

8. Check the well and the sewage system. If the well is shallow you will almost certainly have to drill a new one sometime, and that's expensive. If there's no septic tank you will likely need one.

9. Check the house. You should go over any home you intend to buy with a contractor, but you can get a fair idea yourself of whether you're considering a handyman's delight or the real thing with the help of a couple of small tools — a flashlight, icepick, measuring tape, binoculars, paper and a pencil. Begin in the basement. If it's dry, that's a great start. If the foundation looks like it needs a lot of work, thank the owner and move on. Use the flashlight to check the corners and beams. If the beams appear soft, jab them with the icepick. If you hit solid wood without going in too deep they are likely okay. Check the

wiring. Chances are it will have to be replaced. Have a look at the plumbing. If it isn't copper it will probably have to be replaced, too. Locate the furnace — if there is one. Unless it's hot water or forced air you will likely need a new one. In the living areas pay close attention to the walls. If the plaster sags or has damp spots you will want to replace it with wallboard. Go over the layout using the tape measure and note any load-bearing walls (they usually run at right angles to the support beam, but not always). These can only be removed at tremendous expense. Windows should open and close easily. If there is a fireplace, shine your light up the flue. It should be clear. Ask about insulation: regardless of what you're told you will probably need more.

10. Outside, look at the roof with the binoculars. Unless it seems to be in A-1 shape it will probably need some attention.

11. As you complete this exercise, list all the things the house will require to make it liveable — new roof, wiring, plumbing, furnace, insulation and so on. Take a rough guess at how much it will cost to repair or replace each item. Total the amounts, double the result and add 20% of that total to the asking price and you will have some idea of what paradise will cost you.

12. If country living still appeals to you, make an offer.

## PROPERTY TAXES

Many Canadians year after year continue to pay too much property tax. Different municipalities assess their properties and levy their taxes in different ways. There is very little consistency across the country and, even more important, each assessment method relies heavily on the personal judgment of the assessor.

The result is that many taxpayers are paying either too much or too little property taxes, and the municipality will be only too pleased to adjust them if the true facts are drawn to its attention on a timely basis and an adjustment is warranted.

If you think you've been hit with an unfair property assessment, this is one time when it may be worth your while to fight city hall. You stand an even chance of getting a reduction in assessment on appeal. But the bonus here is the fact that appealing your assessment is free; all it will cost is time and a little leg work.

If you're too busy to spend time researching market values

and documenting an appeal, your spouse or even your older children may be able to do it for you. The fact is that reducing an assessment is relatively straightforward and the chances are you won't need to consult a professional. There are definite steps that you can take yourself to effectively reduce an unfair assessment.

First, make sure your assessment is actually for your property. Strange as it may seem, assessments are sometimes addressed incorrectly or refer to the wrong property.

If it is your assessment, the next step is to check out how your home compares in value with others in the neighborhood. This will take some work on your part, but comparing how your property stacks up with others in the area is the main point of an appeal and is usually well worth the effort.

Here are steps you can take to determine if you've been unfairly assessed:

1. Compile a list of some properties in your area that closely resemble yours. Include in your list those that have the same features as yours, such as a garage, swimming pool, similar size, etc. If similar properties are for sale in your area, all the better. This way you can establish the current market value from your realtor.

2. Visit the local Registry Office and confirm that the information about your property is correctly recorded.

3. Ask the local assessment office for your neighborhood's property rolls. On these rolls you can check out the assessments shown opposite the properties you've listed. Simply write in beside them the sales values.

4. With this information, you should be able to establish assessment ratios to market values which can be compared to the ratio calculated for your property. When you know these ratios you can determine if you have grounds for an appeal. If yours is out of line you've got a good case.

5. Determine if the assessor worked within the rules of the relevant assessment act. This may require the help of a specialist such as a property tax consultant or former assessor who is in business for himself and such services may cost you a lot of money. It's only worth it in extreme cases.

6. Call the district assessment office and arrange an informal meeting with the assessor. If he's made an error, give him the oppor-

tunity to correct it. If the assessment is wrong, the assessor will usually file an amended assessment right away.

By approaching the problem this way, you can avoid spending further time at the appeal stage. But if this negotiation fails, file an appeal.

Count on taking a day off to sit in appeal court prior to your hearing to see what happens; allow yourself another day to collect further data and to attend the appeal itself.

Keep in mind that the appeal court can also raise your taxes as well as lower them, so be sure you have a good case before you go there. Remember, too, that deadline periods for appeals are not flexible; the court will only hear your appeal for the current year's property taxes. This is a very important point to note because the appeal periods are relatively short. Check your assessment notice carefully for the appeal deadline and the address where the appeal must be made.

The appeal process itself is usually pretty straightforward. Start by listing your reasons for appealing on the reverse side of your notice of assessment and send it to the proper authority.

When your appeal date has been set, you can effectively argue your case, if you follow these steps:

1. Take time beforehand to prepare enough copies of your appeal so that all members of the court can follow your argument.
2. Limit your argument to pertinent points. This will retain the attention of the court.
3. Support your case with exhibits, such as charts showing the comparable values of similar homes in your area. Photographs could be helpful, but don't overdo it.
4. Sum up your argument by telling the court what you think the assessment should be — and why.

Even if you are turned down at this level of appeal, you can then go to the provincial court of appeal. But consider this decision carefully. At this point, you become a formal adversary and you'll need a lawyer. What began as a simple free procedure could end up costing you a lot in legal fees.

Nevertheless, the odds of appealing your assessment might be worth the gamble. At least half of all homeowners who appeal effectively chop dollars from their property taxes. And last, but not least, remember there is a principle at stake: why pay the tax-man more than necessary? Remember, a tax dollar saved is a whole dollar.

## SELLING YOUR HOME WITHOUT A BROKER

When you consider that brokerage fees will eat up as much as 6% of your proceeds of sale, it's easy to understand the overwhelming temptation to sell your home privately without the help of a broker or real estate agent. Why, then, do more than 90% of the hundreds of thousands of homes sold in Canada each year go through an agent? Because there's more to selling a house than meets the eye. Let's look more closely at the proposition.

If you act as your own broker, keep in mind that you will have to be patient. It generally takes longer to sell on your own than through an agent, because an agent can reach more potential buyers through widespread advertising and listing services.

Remember, too, you may have to spend anywhere from several hundred to several thousand dollars to entice buyers to your property.

If you decide to sell on your own, begin by making your home as attractive as possible. Nothing turns potential purchasers off more quickly than peeling paint or yesterday's garbage stacked in a corner. Dirty or cracked walls should be replastered or painted; the exterior, too, if it needs it. If the shrubbery or grass on your property is ugly, consider hiring a gardener to get it back in shape.

Once your house is spic and span, there are some steps which will help to close your sale successfully.

1. Set your price, and make it the current market value. Don't overprice. Most vendors arrive at the right figure by checking on other sales in the area or by telephoning real estate agents about advertised listings. Some actually entice agents to their homes for opinions under the pretence of enquiring about a listing. It's likely best to hire a professional appraiser. For a few hundred dollars a professionally qualified appraiser will consider all sales in your area and adjust for any differences between your home and ones that have recently been sold. The appraiser will give you a written report detailing the reasons for arriving at the

price. Don't be shy about using the appraisal as a sales tool. It's an independent valuation. It's also acceptable proof of value to most financial institutions that grant mortgages, an important consideration to possible purchasers.

2. After setting the price, notify the mortgage holder and see if they would be prepared to lend money to a purchaser, how much and on what terms — all necessary information to prospective buyers.

3. Put up a sign. It should be neat and simple. If you are concerned about strangers dropping in at all hours, indicate on the sign "By Appointment." Otherwise, "For Sale" and your telephone number are enough.

4. Your sale will have its widest exposure if you place a classified ad in the newspaper. Count on spending a few hundred dollars if you have to advertise for a long time. Always ask about weekly or monthly rates before placing an ad. The ad should include location, type of house, outstanding features, asking price (raise this if you want to leave room for bargaining) and your phone or box number.

5. Have your lawyer review any offer you are contemplating accepting. Also notify your lawyer of any liens against your property so that arrangements can be made for removing them before your house is sold. A good lawyer will also advise you of any potential flaws in an offer you are considering. Lawyer's fees will vary from transaction to transaction, but fees charged for a relatively simple sale are very reasonable considering the possible costs of a defective sale.

6. When you have cleared a serious offer with your lawyer, consult your mortgage holder to assure everything is in order.

7. Have the purchaser give your lawyer a deposit with the offer (usually half the down payment). Your lawyer will keep it in escrow until the sale is closed. If your buyer fails to come up with the remainder of the down payment, the deposit is usually forfeited.

8. Your lawyer should prepare the mortgage statement, make sure taxes have been paid, arrange for any insurance transfers, and answer questions raised by the buyer. After you have sold your home, your lawyer should also provide you with a written report outlining how the mortgages were settled as well as other details.

When your sign goes up and your advertising campaign is on, expect calls from real estate brokers. They will attempt to persuade you they can sell your home more quickly than you and obtain a better price. Some might even tell you that they have a buyer "looking for a home exactly like yours and willing to pay your price. Just sign this listing statement." Before changing your mind, check with your lawyer.

If you decide to go it alone, not only will you have the satisfaction of knowing that you did it on your own, but you might end up a few thousand dollars richer.

## USING A REAL ESTATE AGENT

On the other hand, most real estate agents are trained to do exactly what you are trying to do — sell your property.

An agent has the resources to provide the widest possible exposure for your house, either through listing your home exclusively with his agency for a particular period of time, or through multiple listing services (M.L.S.). With M.L.S., a description of your house with a picture is sent to all members of your local real estate board. In an exclusive listing you agree to list only with that agent for a specified time and at a specified commission rate.

Whether you sign an exclusive or an M.L.S. listing, take time to check the fine print of your agreement. For instance, under some contracts you will have to pay the agent's commission, even if at the last minute the buyer fails to close the sale. Your best bet is to stick with a contract that allows you to pay your agent's commission only on closing.

What can you expect from your agent in return for the commission? Here are some of the steps a reputable agent should take to sell your house:

1. Get a general appraisal. After investigating your home, a good agent should be able to counsel you on the price you should be looking for and why. But, always remember, it's up to you to set the price.
2. Develop a marketing strategy for selling your home. Your agent should determine what method of exposure will obtain the best results — either an exclusive listing or M.L.S. These plans should be explained to you in detail. He or she should also place classified ads in daily newspapers at his or her firm's expense.

3. Interview prospective buyers on your behalf. Potential purchasers contact your agent directly. The agent should personally
   escort buyers through your property with your consent and at a
   time convenient to you. Your agent is bound by law to present
   every offer to you, even if it is far below your asking price.
   Although no credit check is done on a prospective buyer, your
   agent should qualify potential purchasers by inquiring beforehand into their ability to afford to buy your home. This step
   alone, can save hours of wasted time and much frustration.
4. Negotiate your sale. Although your lawyer will handle most of
   the transaction, your real estate agent can accept a deposit from
   a buyer and keep it in escrow until the purchaser delivers the
   remainder of the down payment and the sale is closed.

## BUYING FOREIGN REAL ESTATE

Often people will buy real estate outside Canada, either as a
straight investment or a place to get away from it all for awhile
every now and then. Even if you know everything there is to know
about Canadian real estate, the minute you step across the border
you're into a whole new ball game. Laws differ, habits change and
there are always problems, and solutions, peculiar to that other
country — even one whose society closely parallels ours. The
United States is no exception.

Here are a few tips to consider when considering the purchase
of foreign real estate.

1. Investigate the developer. A developer's integrity and stability
   are often the most important considerations. Speak with previous customers and take a look at the developer's earlier projects if possible. Check too with state authorities and the U.S.
   Federal Trade Commission (F.T.C.) for outstanding complaints,
   if you are buying property in the United States. If there is no
   Canadian prospectus, inspect a copy of the property report filed
   with the Office of Interstate Land Sales Registration, U.S.
   Department of Housing and Urban Development.
2. Personally inspect your purchase. Nothing beats a first-hand
   look. Pretty photos of a project won't reveal the junkyard or
   expressway behind the camera. Also, investigate such amenities
   as recreation and shopping facilities and medical care.

3. Buy a completed unit. Buying a completed unit saves you from surprises in construction quality, general layout and appearance. The same goes for amenities such as golf courses, clubhouses, yacht clubs and tennis courts. In large development projects, these recreation features may be a year or more from completion.

4. Beware of misleading names. A multinational company's name or initials may be on the prospectus, but it may well have no obligations to guarantee the project. International Telephone and Telegraph (I.T.T.), for instance, had to sign an F.T.C. consent order in which it agreed to "cease and desist" for misrepresenting that it was legally responsible for debts and completion of projects undertaken by I.T.T. Community Development Corp.

5. Obtain legal advice. While some people believe that taking out title insurance, a common practice in the U.S., may eliminate the need for a lawyer's services, this may prove to be penny wise and pound foolish. In any purchase, hiring a lawyer is advisable. Lawyers are trained to read between the lines and track down discrepancies you may miss.

When purchasing property outside the U.S., the same words of caution apply, as well as a few others. You should assess the political situation of a country where you wish to buy property. This, of course, may be tricky, but certainly necessary. Blocked currencies, nationalization, violence and revolution are unpleasant side-effects of buying land in the wrong country.

In any foreign country, including the United States, possible income tax implications should be carefully checked out. Frequently, onerous reporting requirements apply to even owning real estate, let alone buying and selling it.

## RENTAL PROPERTIES

Many people seem to think that buying property to rent is a great way to earn income, but the life of a landlord is not only cashing rent cheques.

Before you rush out to buy a house to rent out, or rent out part of the one you already own, there are a few things to consider.

First of all, you will have to take on the responsibilities and aggravations of being a landlord. Your tenants may enjoy listening to hard rock at full volume or they might like throwing wild parties late into the night — it's often hard to tell when they arrive on your doorstep enquiring about your accommodation for rent. What would you do if their rent cheques started to bounce? Would you evict them? *Could* you evict them? You should find out what your rights are as well as the rights of your tenant. You will probably find out that landlords have almost no rights compared to tenants.

And, what about rent controls? If they apply, forget about being a landlord. In a jurisdiction having rent controls, landlords are soon in a position where they cannot raise their rents sufficiently to cover increased costs of owning and maintaining their buildings. The result is a deterioration in the value of the building and often an absolute loss on the rental operation itself.

Some of these potential problems may be minimized by setting out certain rules in the lease — if you have one — and you should. But, have your lawyer draw your lease to be sure it doesn't contravene any legislation protecting tenants.

You may also run into problems if there is an excess of rental space in your community. You may not be able to keep yours fully occupied. If the conversion of part of your home to an apartment is going to involve considerable expense, you might think twice. If you want to use it again at some time in the future for your own residence you should consider the additional cost of converting back.

In order to ensure you know the result of your rental activity you should set up a separate bank account. All expenses should be paid out of this and all rental payments should be deposited into it. By setting up a simple set of books you will be able to keep track in one place of all your expenses for the year. This will be much easier than trying to remember in December what expenses you paid the previous January.

## MORTGAGES

Still another way to invest in real estate is holding mortgages. But, again, this is not the type of investment that the unsophisticated investor should be considering. Unless you have had considerable experience in the field, or act only after getting competent professional advice on *all* aspects of mortgages, you should leave it to the pros. There are volumes of law applying solely to mortgages. They represent one of the most complex of legal documents and the rights and obligations of holding mortgages can often be a nightmare.

# PART TWO

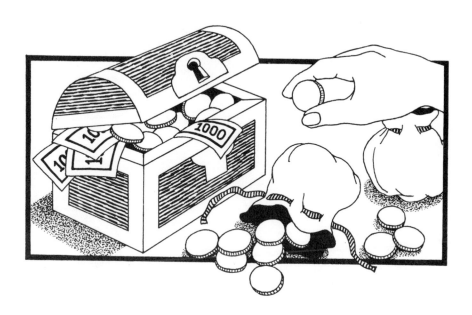

# chapter twelve

# *Introduction to Investment*

You have just completed Part I of this book, a part devoted to money management. Now you are about to begin Part II, which concentrates on investments. Before concluding that Part II isn't relevant to you because you don't view yourself as an investor — or even a potential investor — there are some considerations to take into account. For example, anyone who owns real estate, including the home you live in, is an investor, and if you found the preceding chapter, "Investing In Real Estate" interesting, there is more of the same type of information in the pages following (except that it refers to the stock market). As a matter of fact, the next chapter, "Investment Clubs," outlines a very easy and relatively safe way for inexperienced stock market players to get started.

Another reason to familiarize yourself with Part II is this. Even if you don't have money invested directly in the stock market you are probably still affected by what the market does. If you have an RRSP, a pension plan or an insurance policy, the odds are that some portion of the assets of the institution with which you have your policies or plans are invested in the market, and how the market performs will affect either the value or the cost of your plan or policy, perhaps both. Part II will help you understand how the market works and, in turn, influences your financial affairs, even if indirectly.

Last, and certainly not least, perhaps you *should* have some money invested in the stock market. Part II will help you make that decision. Should the decision be to become a market player you will have a much better chance of protecting your capital and enhancing your investment income if you read on.

# chapter thirteen
# *Investment Clubs*

## WHAT, WHY, AND HOW

Groups of interested individuals often get together in order to pool their funds and invest in the stock market. That's your basic investment club.

People form these investment clubs for a variety of reasons. Perhaps the members don't have enough money available individually to invest themselves. Since it is necessary to have at least hundreds, if not thousands, of dollars available to take advantage of the yields offered by some securities (as well as to reduce brokerage fees), club members may decide to combine their money with that of friends in order to be able to play the game. It is also a good way to invest in a diversified portfolio without having a lot of cash. As individuals, they may not be able to build up enough cash to purchase shares in more than one company or industry. As a group, there may not be a problem spreading the risk around a bit.

Perhaps they simply want to gain experience in the stock market without risking a great deal of their own money. By investing a small amount periodically they can discuss investments with a group of other interested people and in this way learn how to evaluate investment opportunities.

Perhaps the individuals involved may not have had very much experience handling money. For example, a housewife whose husband handles all the family finances would, as a member of an investment club, learn about making monetary decisions. This would help stand her in good stead if she was suddenly put in the position of having to manage the family finances by herself.

An investment club is also a good way to develop an awareness of our economy and the many forces that affect it. In today's unsettled economic times it is comforting to be at least aware something is happening even if you don't fully understand what's going on.

Finally, an individual may want to make some money. This point should not be played down. By investing carefully it is possible to make money in an investment club, either by holding securities that earn income or by trading them to realize capital gains. After all, joining an investment club could be an expensive lesson if the only thing gained was experience.

Whatever the reason for forming it, the concept of an investment club is basically simple. Each member of the club contributes a lump sum amount at the beginning, regular amounts on a periodic basis, or a combination of the two. Then as enough cash is built up, the investment committee, which could consist of one member, the entire club, or anything in between, studies the market in order to find the securities that best fit the club's objectives and philosophy. When the securities are chosen, the committee, or its delegate, contacts a broker who will complete the transaction. As income is received, or capital gains or losses realized, the transactions are recorded. Each year annual returns are filed with Revenue Canada reporting the income or losses of the members. Of course, the income or loss is allocated to the members and paid out or absorbed according to the club rules.

That sounds pretty straightforward. But, before you run out and form a club, a number of important points should be carefully considered.

## Income Tax

There are a number of specific income tax rules that apply to investment clubs and professional advice should always be sought before embarking on this type of venture, and once in operation you should always keep up-to-date on income tax changes.

## Make Rules

As investors, you should carefully consider what the ground rules will be for the operation of the club. If you are going to have one person making the investment decisions, then he or she should report on each trade made; or if a committee is struck to perform this function, it should have a set voting procedure to avoid squabbles.

It is essential that the amount and timing of cash contributions be decided in advance. Otherwise control is lost over the amount of new investment that can be made on a regular basis.

Along the same lines, you have to decide whether any income earned in the club can be withdrawn or must be re-invested.

Perhaps the most important ground rule of all is to decide how new members are to be admitted and how members who want to leave can get their money out.

## Philosophy

Next comes the question of the club's philosophy. This is probably the most difficult area to decide since each member will have his or her own opinion. However, it is essential that each member of the club have the same investment goals and risk/return levels. Conflicts will inevitably arise if some members want to buy stocks on margin or borrow from the bank while others want to reduce their risk and simply invest money contributed or earned in the club. Also, some may want to invest in high-risk, speculative securities in order to make a quick capital gain while others may be content to buy blue chip securities in order to protect their capital and at the same time earn some income.

If these issues are not considered and resolved before the club is formed and money is contributed, you can be sure they will come up in the near future — and when their own money is at stake your erstwhile friends may not be so easy to get along with.

## Valuing the Interest

The question of the value of an interest in an investment club usually comes into prominence at two points in time. First, when a new member is admitted, and next when an existing member wants to get out. In each case the fair market value of the club's assets has to be arrived at.

Although this calculation can be done anytime, it's easiest to do at the end of a natural reporting period, such as the end of the month.

Financial statements should be prepared regularly. If members contribute on a weekly or monthly basis and the amounts vary, then statements should be prepared monthly to take into account fluctuations in the value of securities held. If each member contributes the same amount each period and no one joins or leaves the club, then quarterly or yearly statements may suffice. How often statements are prepared really depends on the level of activity and the personal desires of the members.

The following steps are necessary to arrive at a value for each member's interest in the club:

- Record the initial cash input by each member.
- Determine the proportionate share of the initial contribution paid by each member.
- Invest that money in securities.
- Add new contributions by each individual to their respective share of the total initial contribution.
- Invest these new contributions.
- Record income or losses realized.
- Record any amounts paid out to members.
- At the end of the accounting period calculate the market value of the net assets held in the club.
- Determine each member's share of this value based on his or her share of the value at the end of the prior period plus cash contributions since, less any amounts withdrawn.

This calculation determines the value of the holding of each individual member. It may sound complicated, but in order to take into account different proportionate shares in the club, changes in the value of the securities held, withdrawals, and varying contributions over the period, this calculation is necessary to arrive at a fair market value for each member's share.

Before an individual can buy into or withdraw from the club a calculation such as the one above has to be made. On joining the club the individual would make a cash contribution and the proportion that this cash contribution is of the new market value of the club would be his or her proportionate share in the value of the club. A member may feel that he or she should receive a higher interest in the club to take into account the fact that some of the securities held may have unrecognized capital gains with an underlying tax liability to each member which should be adjusted for. This is another club rule for you to decide. Rather than adjusting for it, you may feel that this is an appropriate initiation fee. On the other hand, if there is an unrealized capital loss, the existing members may feel that new members should pay more if they will be able to claim their proportion of the losses on their personal tax returns in the year the securities are sold. The same line of reasoning can be made for possible adjustments due to accrued interest or declared but unpaid dividends at the date someone leaves or joins. The point is, the club as a whole must decide these issues ahead of time.

The situation is a little different when club assets have to be disposed of to pay off a member who is leaving. Should the departing member be allocated a proportion (calculated prior to the redemption of the share) of any capital gain realized on the liquidation of the club assets in order to share the tax burden? Since the departing member caused the problem in the first place you may feel he or she should help pay for it. If you decide that the member should help pay for it, then he or she will get an appropriate share of any capital gain. If, on the other hand, a capital loss is realized on the liquidation of assets, that share should probably be allocated as well.

Another way to deal with shares in an investment club is by buying and selling between individuals. In this way the club itself is not affected. The new member simply takes over the old member's proportionate share in the club. Any gain or loss to the vendor on the sale is not calculated based on his or her share of the market value. It is based on the cost base of the investment at the time of the sale.

Another important ground rule is the determination of the method of allocating income among members. This rule basically falls out of the determination of the value of each member's interest in the club. Income or losses can be allocated at the end of each accounting period based on each member's proportionate share in the current value of the club. For example, if someone's share of the club is 10% he or she would be allocated 10% of all interest, 10% of all dividends and 10% of all capital gains or losses.

As you can see, the ground rules for an investment club are not simple. However, a workable system must be pounded out. Since the success of the club depends on it, it is worth the extra care involved.

## More Philosophy

Other important philosophical issues must be dealt with before an investment club begins operating, issues which will have a definite impact on the eventual success of the club, from both an economic and a human relations point of view.

And these issues are often the most difficult to resolve. Because they relate to personal values and objectives, most are not easily quantified, measured or reduced to hard and fast, written rules of operation. On the other hand, there are some which are quantifiable, but usually the quantity determined to be right is arbitrarily set.

To avoid some of the possible conflicts which may otherwise come up during the lifetime of the club, it is important that the majority of these issues, too, be resolved before the actual operations of the club begin. In this way, if disagreements arise, any members who wish to leave can do so without creating some of the problems discussed above regarding valuations, etc.

One of the first issues to be resolved is the atmosphere under which the club will be operating. If it is going to be primarily a social club, where people are involved because they have a general interest in investments but also want to meet with their friends on a regular basis, then some of the investment decisions may not be as carefully thought out as they should be. But then, that may not be essential to these people. If, on the other hand, the club will be operated as a business, the investment decisions may be sound but there may not be enough socializing to satisfy some members.

In order for a club to be successful in the long run, it is necessary for the members to assess themselves, as well as the rest of the group, to find out if there is a match. It isn't necessary that everyone think exactly the same. In fact, it may be the best if they don't. Those people who are keenly interested in the business aspect can form the core of the investment committee and ensure that good, sound decisions are reached. Those who joined because of the good times as well as an interest in investment, can arrange the meetings, look after administration and keep morale high. The danger lies in the extremes — all work or all play — since these may lead to early conflicts or dissatisfaction.

Once the atmosphere has been established, you have to decide how much money is to be contributed and when. The choices range from one large sum to small amounts regularly, or a combination of the two. The decision, to a certain extent, will be based on where the club lies between a purely social club and a business club. If the club is all social and general interest then the contributions may be kept low to reduce the amount of money at risk. If it is all business then the amount may be high in order to build up a large amount of capital as quickly as possible. It isn't necessary that each member contribute the same amount, but it does make the bookkeeping easier.

One of the most important decisions to be faced by your group is the determination of your investment goals. Somehow you have to decide whether you are going to invest for the short- or long-term and what level of risk you are willing to accept. This is where the fun begins. In order to invest for short-term gains you will look for the quick capital gain to be made on special information or sound reasoning, or you will look for the securities paying higher than normal income yields. In either case, this type of activity normally carries with it a higher degree of risk, especially if your group is inexperienced. By looking at long-term investments, for either capital appreciation or income yields, you do not necessarily eliminate your risk. Many stocks, even over the long run, prove to be losers. By investing in blue-chip securities you can reduce the amount of risk involved but this may also reduce the members' degree of interest in the club.

Whichever decision is made, long- or short-term, it is important that you do your homework before investing. Talk to your stockbroker, read the financial press, listen to economic forecasts and do anything else you can think of to find out more about your potential investments before you pay out the cash.

Speaking of cash, you must decide whether or not you are going to use any form of borrowed money to invest. Again, this decision will be based on the amount of risk your group is willing to assume. In a period of rising prices, leverage (using other people's money) will increase your gains above those which you normally would have enjoyed. However, in a period of falling prices, this same tool will increase your losses above the level you would otherwise have experienced. In addition, with today's volatile interest rates, you would have to ensure there is enough cash on hand in the club to meet the monthly interest charges. As a result, someone always has to watch the cash flow carefully in order to avoid missing an interest payment.

One other point which should be discussed at the start is the size of the club. Some may want to keep it to a group of close friends, say, ten, while others may want to let it get up to thirty or forty in order to build up the cash base from which to invest. This decision should take into account the extra bookkeeping and paperwork involved. You could also run into the problem of where to hold the meetings. In addition, when new people are added, you would have to ensure that they have the same goals and objectives as the original group. Otherwise, these new members could over-rule your previous decisions as to ground rules and philosophy. The numbers question becomes increasingly important once you begin to approach people who are not close friends. At that time you should contact your provincial securities commission to see whether or not you will be considered to be making a public issue of securities. As you can see, big is not necessarily best, especially since your share of the income will remain the same in terms of absolute dollars.

The resolution of these issues will not guarantee the eventual success of your club. However, by dealing with them early, you will at least have cleared the air of questions on how the club will operate. You can then concentrate on fulfilling your objective for joining the club.

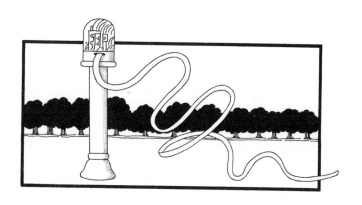

# chapter fourteen

# *Investing in Securities*

You do not have to be a Rockefeller or a Bay Street denizen to invest in the stock market. As you will see as you read on, there is a place in the market for investors of all sizes and attitudes. Indeed, as pointed out in Chapter 12, the market affects the financial affairs of most of us even if we don't own stocks or bonds directly. This is so because nearly every institution that we deal with — banks, trust companies, insurance companies; and their plans and policies — rely in large part on investments in the stock market for income, either in the form of capital gains or dividends.

As a matter of fact, you don't invest in the stock market at all. When you buy a share or a bond you are investing in the corporation that issued the share or bond. The "market" is just the store at which you bought it, and where you sell it later.

Of course we all know of people who have been badly burned "in the market" and there's no denying that happens. But I don't know of any endeavour that's completely safe. A good friend of mine broke her hip the other day going to church.

An understanding of how the market works to affect the value of your investment (which this part of the book will give you), combined with a good dose of common sense, will go a long way to helping you make money by investing in securities.

The word "securities" is used here to mean stocks and bonds traded on the stock markets. Although in recent years investment attitudes have favoured everything from real estate to precious metals and art, you should always consider the stock market as a place to invest.

Remember that it isn't important what the "market" is doing — what counts is what *your* investments are doing. As one investment house correctly stated in its advertisements a few years ago: "Asking how the stock market is doing is like asking what the weather is like in North America."

Carefully chosen securities offer as much protection of capital as do most real estate investment opportunities which are realistically available to the general public. You must always remember that there are many, many corporations and individuals who are actively involved in the business of investing in real estate. They usually take up the vast majority of large, direct real estate investment opportunities. So, what's left over for the general public are usually high risk ventures which, from an investment standpoint, are probably not as safe as blue-chip stocks. Because most of us have seen residential real estate, as well as commercial real estate, in certain high-growth areas continue to increase in value in leaps and bounds, we tend to look upon all real estate as a perfectly safe investment. This is simply not the case. You can lose money investing in real estate — especially, as already mentioned, if you sink your money into the left-overs that the professional real estate investors consider to be too high-risk to fund completely themselves. And continuity of a reasonable income from investments in many securities is an advantage not always available from investments in real estate.

For example, the Bank of Montreal has paid dividends on its common shares every year since 1828. The Bank of Nova Scotia has paid dividends on its common shares every year since 1833. A reasonable annual rate of return is obtainable by investing in top-quality securities. On the other hand, vacant cottage lots will not produce annual income, which might be more important to you than the future capital gains.

Considering the preferential income tax treatment given to income from Canadian securities (particularly dividends), the insidious and seemingly never-ending increases in property taxes, and the rent control mentality of many provincial governments, it's not always easy to find an after-tax return from rental real estate comparable to that available from top-quality stocks and bonds.

Although bonds do not provide much of a hedge against inflation, good quality shares often do. Those who feel that only real estate is a reasonable hedge against decreases in the purchasing power of the dollar might ask their brokers to provide them with a list of stocks whose values have more than kept pace with inflation. Yes, they do exist.

A major advantage attached to investments in securities is the ability to invest as much or as little as one pleases. There is literally no upper limit and one can invest as little as a few hundred dollars in stocks or bonds.

Then there is the almost instant marketability of all or a part of your securities to meet emergencies or planned major expenditures. This marketability feature affords excellent flexibility in being able to adjust your holdings in accordance with changed investment objectives, fluctuating market conditions vis-à-vis particular securities, or their underlying attractiveness.

Investments in securities are easy to manage and publicly-traded securities can be realistically valued immediately, except in very unusual circumstances, by referring to the financial press. Contrast this feature of investments in publicly-traded securities with the difficulty, cost and range of results of real estate appraisals.

It must be emphasized now that these comments are not in any way intended to detract from the many, and very real, attractive features of real estate as an investment, but rather are meant to call attention to the advantages of investment in securities — advantages which are often overlooked or not given adequate consideration by many investors. Real estate investments are dealt with in Chapter 11. Meanwhile, back to some more advantages of investing in publicly traded stocks and bonds.

There is always the possibility of investment growth in the form of the receipt of rights which can be sold to realize a pure profit or exercised to obtain additional shares at a reduced cost. Then there is the additional possibility of shares being split. This usually results in growth of the holder's original investment.

Finally, there exists the chance that one corporation may want to acquire control of another, a situation normally accompanied by a favourable price being offered to the shareholders of the corporation which is being taken over. From time to time there are epidemics of takeover attempts, admittedly to the chagrin of some, but nonetheless to the advantage of many, shareholders.

In addition to the foregoing, many investors gain a great deal of satisfaction from their active participation in a corporation's growth. The fact remains, too, that investment in stocks and debt of corporations is desperately needed in order to continue adequate development of our country and its very impressive resources.

There is a lot to be said for investing in securities. From a nationalistic point of view, a continuing problem is that our country needs more investment. From a business standpoint, there is a shortage of investment funds. Finally, from a strictly selfish attitude, there is the continuing opportunity to make money in the stock market. To repeat, it doesn't really matter how the "market" is doing — what's important is how *your* stocks and bonds are doing.

The next few chapters are designed to help you better understand just how the stock market works. They will also point out and explain some of the most important elements you should be familiar with before committing funds to the market. I refer you now to the "Investment Glossary" found in the back of this book. Some of these terms, particularly those from the legal and accounting worlds, have general meanings apart and often different from their specialized meanings as applied within the investment business, so it is important to read through the glossary at this point, and refer to it whenever helpful.

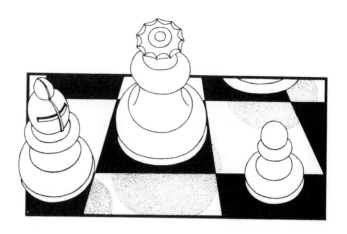

# chapter fifteen

# *Types of Market Players*

## THE THREE TYPES

Once you are convinced that the stock market is a viable investment vehicle, the first thing you have to decide, even before con-
tacting a broker, is what kind of market player you are going to be.
Even the Canadian Securities Institute, the educational organization of the Investment Dealers Association of Canada and the
major stock exchanges, characterize three distinct classifications
of market players. They are the investor, the speculator and the
gambler. The reason you have to classify yourself is to determine
the type of investments which will form the bulk of your activity.

Following is an examination of the characteristics of each of
the three types of market players.

### The Real Investor

Time is an important factor to the real investor. Generally speaking, the real investor adopts a longer-term view of things than the
speculator, who in turn takes a longer-term view of things than
does the gambler. The hallmark of the investor is patience. The
real investor invests capital to produce a regular income as well as
a capital gain over a period of years. The main concern of the real

investor is safety of capital followed closely by regularity of income. Good credit risks only are selected, with the favourite purchase being a security of a company with a good record, a good reputation and a solid, promising future. When the real investor buys an industrial issue it's an established company with a good history. The real investor demands evidence of earning power and asset values and looks for a reasonable margin of safety in both.

The real investor never buys securities at random, doesn't invest with borrowed money (unless assured of a higher return than the cost of borrowing on an after-tax basis) and works toward definite investment objectives by following a long-term, well-thought-out, investment plan.

## The Speculator

The speculator is a different breed altogether. He is impatient and adopts a much shorter view than the investor. The speculator is continually on the lookout for securities which are undervalued in relation to short-term prospects. He takes calculated risks and seeks his reward in the form of quick capital gains rather than regular income or long-term appreciation. He is quite prepared to accept a capital loss when he guesses wrong.

But, it should be recognized that the speculator is not necessarily to be branded a non-desirable. Speculators perform two very useful services. They tend to level out what would otherwise be great swings in prices by buying when prices are depressed and selling when prices are rising, and they are also a source of risk capital. Intelligent speculation may quite properly form part of the investment program of some investors.

The main point is to understand the difference between investing and speculating and to know which you are doing. It could be disastrous to think you are investing when in fact you are speculating.

## The Gambler

A completely different kind of cat. The gambler bets on the unknown by acting on hunches and tips rather than on carefully studied data. His trademark is buying long shots in the hope of making a killing — quick or otherwise.

The gambler normally appears on the scene after the stock

market has enjoyed a period of rising prices and volume. He hears about people making money in the market and wants to get a piece of this — to him — easy money. The gambler, though, is usually not prepared to go to the trouble of getting the facts about his "investments." Normally he knows only what he hears, and usually what he hears are rumours and tips passed on by people as poorly informed as he is. It's possible to conceive of the gambler acting on a rumour he started himself.

Other characteristics of the gambler include: operating on limited capital; generally prospering only while the market is buoyant; being caught totally unprepared when the inevitable downturn comes; selling at a loss; and blaming others for his troubles.

The gambler should stick to buying lottery tickets.

## INVESTMENT VS SPECULATION

Remember that the distinction between investment and speculation is clearly one of quality rather than one of form. Either bonds or shares might be suitable as either investments or speculations. The definition becomes a function of determining the quality of security before purchasing it by investigating the relevant facts. Later on some advice will be given as to how to go about this.

All the securities available form a broad spectrum ranging from top-quality, high-grade investments all the way down to out-right gambles. There is no clear-cut dividing line anywhere on this spectrum between investment and speculative securities — just degrees of each type.

There are some general rules of thumb, though.

Government and municipal bonds are seldom, if ever, speculative. If they are not in default, and have no unfavourable history of defaults of interest or principal, they are usually considered to be of investment quality.

When it comes to corporate bonds, a number of tests have been devised to measure their investment calibre and, as mentioned, these will be dealt with later. Suffice for now to say that such tests are largely measures of safety of principal and certainty of income. In short, the hallmarks of investment quality corporation bonds are consistent earning power and adequate underlying assets.

There have also been a number of tests devised for measuring the investment quality of stocks. They are considered investment prospects rather than speculatives if they have a trend of strong earnings, have paid regular dividends for a number of years, and have all the appearances of carrying on these traditions.

We have to examine investment objectives in a little more depth before moving on to other detailed aspects of investing in securities.

# chapter sixteen
# *Investment Objectives*

## SETTING GOALS

Unless you have specific goals in mind it is very difficult to build a successful and appropriate portfolio.

Of course, investment objectives vary from person to person. One person may be mostly interested in protecting his or her capital, another in earning income to live on. Someone else might be primarily concerned with capital growth, perhaps to live on the income therefrom in retirement. The point is you must decide what your objectives are before you even pick a broker.

### Security of Capital

Individuals who are dependent on investments for all or most of their income need a high level of safety and price stability. The same holds true for people who are, in effect, setting up a fund to meet some future need, such as children's education, future care of a disabled dependent, or retirement.

Maximum safety is found in securities such as Canada Savings Bonds and high-quality preferred shares. Blue chip common stocks may well have a place in this type of portfolio, but probably not if *short-term* price stability is a major criterion.

## Income

It is well known that the higher the yield the greater the risk. When income is the main objective — or ranks equally with security of capital, which is often the case — a balanced portfolio is usually preferable. This would be a portfolio consisting primarily of short-term government bonds, high-quality preferred shares and blue chip common stocks with a good dividend record.

## Capital Gain

When growth of capital in the form of appreciation in the value of the portfolio is the main objective, then common shares are the way to go. This is usually the objective of the investor who has enough annual income to meet current living costs, but wants his or her capital to grow to meet future needs, such as retirement or children's education. Also, investors who would prefer to pay tax later on a capital gain  rather than now on interest or dividends should look for growth situations. The longer you can put off paying a tax, the less it costs in real terms; furthermore, your tax rate will probably be lower during retirement than when working full-time. But, not just any old common shares will do. A happy medium must be struck. What has to be found is that elusive investment known as the growth company.

In this context a growth company is one whose common shares have maintained an above-average rate of growth over a period of five years or more and are likely to continue to do so. The increase in price must be the result of permanent factors such as good profits, increasing value of assets, adequate working capital and above-average return on equity. Anything else is not growth investment, it's speculation.

Growth companies usually are characterized by a high rate of earnings on capital invested, a high level of retention and reinvestment of earnings as opposed to a high dividend payment (although some growth companies do pay nominal dividends), capable and dynamic management, and an above-average opportunity for increased earnings, such as a technological competitive edge.

A real growth company should have an above-average rate of earnings on its invested capital over at least a five-year period. It should also appear reasonable to expect that the company will be able to maintain a similar or better rate on additional invested capital. The real test is increasing unit and dollar sales over a reasonable number of years combined with a firm control of costs.

Characteristically, real growth companies finance a major part of expansion out of retained earnings. The company with above-average sales and earnings which are all paid out in dividends, or a company that increases capital through outside financing as quickly as earnings expand, is not a real growth company, but it's probably an excellent choice for the investor who is looking for a mix of income and *some* growth. Growth companies usually have a conservative dividend policy.

Another characteristic of the real growth company is competent and dynamic — even aggressive — management. Growth companies tend to spend a lot of money on research and development. As a matter of fact, a detailed study by the Stanford Research Institute of the relative post-war growth of 400 corporations revealed that high growth companies were predominately research and development oriented. That, of course, is not surprising.

But, it's also not enough. Emphasis must also be placed on merchandising, advertising, public relations, cost control, product management and personnel management and development, as well as on product research and development.

The opportunity for earnings growth is often greater in young, expanding industries. The opportunity may exist in the form of key patent or copyright ownership. Sometimes it's in the form of management which consistently recognizes and capitalizes on new opportunities before their competitors do.

## Caveat Emptor

Never is the adage "let the buyer beware" more appropriate than in the purchase of growth stocks. Ideally a growth stock should be purchased in the early stages of its growth cycle. Because growth stocks tend to have low yields, you must guard against paying prices which have already taken into account most of the expected growth.

It's impossible to have the ultimate in capital security, income and growth potential at the same time. Your investment portfolio must be designed to attach the right degree of importance to each objective based on your particular circumstances.

Having decided what type of investor you are and what your investment objectives will be, the next steps are to open an account and to choose a broker.

# chapter seventeen

# *Operating an Account*

If you're going to invest in Canada securities by playing the stock market you should open an account with a broker who is subject to the regulations of the various stock exchanges and the Investment Dealers Association of Canada.

For your safety, these regulations require investment dealers to: maintain adequate capital in their businesses; carry extensive insurance; maintain proper accounting control and supervision over employees; and, be subject to independent audits. Furthermore, the Investment Dealers Association and the Toronto, Montreal, Canadian and Vancouver stock exchanges have established a national contingency fund. Payments from this fund may be authorized to help investors who suffer losses from the financial failure of a member.

All accounts are handled by professionally trained and licensed representatives who buy and sell on your behalf. The representative's services will be available on a personal, confidential basis, and although he or she is not an investment counsellor per se, your representative can help you make your investment decisions.

We should pause for a moment here to consider a relatively new development in Canada. On April 1, 1983, the rules for buying and selling stocks were changed to allow brokers to negotiate the amount of commission charged to clients rather than having to stick to a prescribed rate schedule.

This change resulted in the establishment of no-frills broker-age houses which simply execute your order, and because they offer no other services whatsoever, are able to charge a lower commission than the conventional, established firms which have large research departments, underwriting facilities and the like, and the brokers who offer advice to clients when asked.

The question, of course, is should investors place their orders where the commission is lowest, or should they deal with the firms offering the broader range of services even if it costs them more to do so.

Unless you are the type of investor who knows exactly what to buy, when to buy, and when to sell, you will probably be better off with the larger, non-discount broker.

The higher commission, for most market players, will be more than offset by the availability of information about investments; access to blocks of stock and new issues; the more efficient execution of trades; stability of the firm; and most important of all, the knowledge your broker has about you. Your broker should be looked upon no differently than your doctor, lawyer, accountant, or any other professional advisor. He or she should be completely familiar with your investment goals, your resources, and the type of investments that you will be comfortable with.

When an account is opened, in addition to the usual information such as name, address, occupation, bank references, etc., the broker will want to know about your financial circumstances, your investment objectives, and details of any securities you already own.

The most common type of account opened is a cash account. This means that you pay in full for securities bought, or deliver securities sold, by the settlement date (usually the fifth day after the date of the transaction).

Another type of account is the margin account, which works generally as follows. Stocks, but not penny stocks, may be purchased on margin, meaning that cash equal to at least 50% of the purchase prices is put up by you with the balance being borrowed from the broker. Of course, interest must be paid on this loan. Also, if the value of the stock declines, you will have to put up more cash because the amount of the loan cannot exceed 50% of the

**FIGURE 2   Sample Confirmation Slip for Purchase of Shares**

Name of investment firm ⟶

Date transaction was made ⟶

# ABC SECURITIES LIMITED

MR. J. LYMAN MAC INNIS, C.A.
TOUCHE ROSS & CO.
P.O. BOX 12
FIRST CANADIAN PLACE
TORONTO ONTARIO
M5X 1B3

**Date**          11 APR 1983
**Account**      J. SCHULTZ
**Executive**
**Client No.**    12345
**Order No.**     678

Broker's name ⟶

AS AGENTS, WE HAVE TODAY BOUGHT FOR YOUR ACCOUNT

| NUMBER OF SHARES | | |
|---|---|---|
| **Bought** | **Sold** | |
| 1,000 | | COMPUTALOG GEARHART LTD<br>COMMON |

| **Shares** | **Price** | **Principal Amount** | **Commission** | **Market** |
|---|---|---|---|---|
| 1,000 | 6.50 | 6,500.00 | 175.85 | TSE |

Indicates stock market on which shares are traded. "TSE" means Toronto Stock Exchange.

Amount you must pay by settlement date. Is cost of shares plus commission.

| Settlement<br>Date | Settlement<br>Amount |
|---|---|
| 18 APR<br>83 | 6,675.85 |

PLEASE COMPLETE THIS TRANSACTION BY THE                    E & O E
SETTLEMENT DATE SHOWN

Date by which you must pay the "Settlement Amount" to the investment firm. Also, the actual date of purchase or sale for income tax purposes.

Means "errors and omissions excepted." A legal term which warns you that errors can be corrected and the transaction will have to be settled as it actually took place.

**FIGURE 3** **Sample Confirmation Slip for Sale of Shares**

## ABC SECURITIES LIMITED

MR. J. LYMAN MAC INNIS, C.A.  **Date** 04 MAR 1983
TOUCHE ROSS & CO.  **Account** J. SCHULTZ
P.O. BOX 12  **Executive**
FIRST CANADIAN PLACE  **Client No.** 12345
TORONTO, ONTARIO  **Order No.** 678
M5X 1B3

AS AGENTS, WE HAVE TODAY SOLD FOR YOUR ACCOUNT

| NUMBER OF SHARES | | |
|---|---|---|
| **Bought** | **Sold** | |
| | 500 | CANADA TRUSTCO MORTGAGE CO<br>SERIES G WARRANTS EXP 02/10/87 |

| Shares | Price | Principal Amount | Commission | Market |
|---|---|---|---|---|
| 500 | 17.00 | 8,500.00 | 185.00 | TSE |

Proceeds of sale less commission

| Settlement Date | Settlement Amount |
|---|---|
| 11 MAR 83 | 8,315.00 |

PLEASE COMPLETE THIS TRANSACTION BY THE  E & O E
SETTLEMENT DATE SHOWN

See additional explanations
on Figure 2.

market value of the relevant stock. As a matter of fact, depending on the circumstances, sometimes the percentage is higher than 50%. So check it out.

After an account has been opened with a broker, orders can be placed either in writing or orally. Brokers are usually happy to provide up-to-the-minute bids and ask quotations for their clients on any publicly traded stock or bond.

When an order is executed, your broker will mail you a written confirmation — usually on the same day. You then have evidence in writing of exactly what has been bought or sold, the price paid or received, the commission charges (or accrued interest where applicable), and the net cost or proceeds. See figures 2 and 3 for sample confirmation slips. If you bought a security, the broker will debit the cost and charges against any funds you may have on deposit with the broker, otherwise you will have to pay the broker by the fifth business day after the transaction. If you sold a security, you would have to deliver the shares sold, in negotiable form, no later than the fifth business day after the transaction — unless, of course, the shares were already held for safekeeping by the broker. If you made a sale, depending entirely on your wishes, the broker will either send you a cheque or keep the funds on deposit for you. Interest is earned by you on funds left on deposit with your broker.

If the security sold is registered in your name, you must sign your name on the back of the certificate in exactly the same way as it appears on the front, date it, and have your signature witnessed. If it is jointly held, all joint holders must endorse it. If you have certificates which were previously duly endorsed, they are already negotiable; in effect they are bearer certificates. Bearer certificates need not be endorsed; they are negotiable by delivery. Securities purchased will also be in either registered or bearer form.

The names and addresses of the owners of securities in registered form are kept on record by the security issuer who will mail any interest, dividends, and shareholder information to the registered holders. Should you change your address while owning a registered security you should notify the transfer agent, whose name is usually shown on the certificate, so that mail may be redirected. A registered security may be registered in the owner's name, in a nominee's name or in "street" (broker's) name. For convenience in handling, many securities are registered in nominee or street name.

A bearer security is negotiable in the same way as money. The holder of a bearer security — that is, the person in possession of it — is presumed to be the owner. Accordingly, if bearer securities are stolen or lost, it is easy for a thief to turn them into cash. Bearer bonds have numbered and dated interest coupons attached and arranged in convenient order for clipping. As each coupon becomes due it should be clipped and cashed at any chartered bank or your brokers' office.

Interest or dividends on securities the broker holds on your behalf will be sent directly to you by the issuer's transfer agent if the securities are registered in your name. If they are not in your name you should check your monthly broker statement to ensure that your account has been credited by the broker with any amounts you are entitled to.

At the end of each month your broker will send you a statement of transactions during the month, showing any credit or debit balance outstanding on securities transacted or held on your behalf. The confirmation slips and monthly statements provide a valuable check to ensure that your records agree with your broker's. Any discrepancies should be called to the broker's attention immediately.

It is also a good idea to retain all confirmations and statements for tax and investment management purposes. Most brokers will provide you with year-end summaries, but it's best to maintain your own separate check.

However, you're not yet ready to call a broker. Read on.

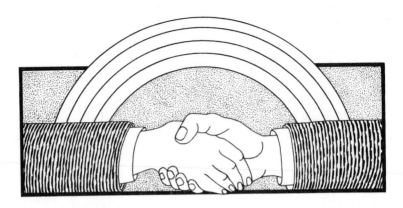

## chapter eighteen

# *Choosing and Dealing With a Broker*

## GIVE IT THOUGHT

Many investors give less time and thought to selecting a broker than they do to buying a newspaper. Although most people who play the market are by nature somewhat cynical (particularly if they have been in it longer than six months), it is surprising how many share the naive assumption that most of the thousands of men and women who sell stocks are more or less equal in their knowledge, honesty and ability to separate the wheat from the chaff in the contradictory information and hearsay that constantly surrounds all stocks.

They are not.

Many are outstanding. Some, while honest, are so inept they should be in other businesses. The majority, however, as in any other profession, are capable. And, in fact, the average broker today is better trained and better motivated than the average broker of twenty years ago, when many of them were attracted to the business by visions of quick killings amid the excesses of a speculative market.

The sad truth is many investors who have had bad experiences in the market can justifiably attribute their losses, in part, to relying on brokers who are more interested in making a commission than helping their clients. Although, in fairness, you must always remember that brokers make their money buying and selling securities, not by advising you what to do. But, you can still make good and bad choices of brokers.

Unfortunately, there are no guidelines guaranteed to help you select the right broker. The choice is very subjective and made even more complicated by the fact there is no simple way to evaluate a broker's handling of your account. Nonetheless, the decision of who should be handling your portfolio should, like all investment decisions, be reassessed from time to time, simply as a precaution to ensure that your needs are being met.

In selecting a broker, the first thing you should do is ask yourself honestly what it is you want out of the market, remembering that the level of return will depend on the degree of risk. Determine how much of your time you are willing to spend analyzing investments; and don't expect a lot of attention from a broker if your total portfolio is worth a couple of thousand dollars. Some firms discourage their sales personnel from taking on accounts that will deal in, what is to them, nuisance-size orders. Others, however, take the attitude that all accounts are worthwhile because they grow over time.

If your age and income indicate that a conservative portfolio consisting of bonds, preferred shares and blue chip stocks for income is in order, then you are probably best off dealing with one of the really big brokerage houses. They are best suited to provide you with large allotments of the low risk, new issues that are suitable for your type of portfolio.

But even then you must find an individual within the firm who is willing to provide you with information pertinent to your particular needs and to advise you on portfolio changes, if necessary.

If your portfolio is large and broadly diversified, and you want conservatism, then you will want to deal with a firm that offers a portfolio review service.

It comes down to picking a firm that can provide you with the services that are most suited to your investment philosophy, and an individual who can and will give you the personal service and guidance consistent with your objectives.

Many investors simply accept their broker's recommendations without question, failing to realize that many brokers do not analyze the securities they sell. The really good broker will do more than quote a few platitudes from a promotional blurb. He or she will give you detailed information which will enable you to determine whether a particular investment meets your particular needs.

Look at the reputation of the brokerage firm and ask to see the type of information it produces for its clients to determine if its recommendations are sent to all investors at the same time. You don't want information a week after the firm's largest clients have had it.

The final decision on a purchase or sale is yours. Still, you may rely heavily on the broker for advice, so it is imperative that you determine how a specific recommendation was arrived at. It is your money that is at risk.

Always remember that the individual broker you deal with is more important to you than his or her firm's reputation as a whole. However, the firm's research capability and method of distributing information to clients like you are also key considerations.

A good broker should be willing to take the time necessary to tailor an investment program to your individual needs. Ask the broker what the typical clients' investment activity is: that is, the amount of money they have invested, how often they buy and sell, and the types of securities they deal in. If it's way out of line with your circumstances you probably should look elsewhere.

It's also a good idea to have a face-to-face meeting with any brokers you are considering. Actually, some brokerage houses insist on such meetings to determine what is a suitable investment level for the client and whether the client can afford them.

If you have never opened an account with a broker be prepared to answer a lot of questions about your net worth and other financial information. A broker is almost certain to check out your bank references and will probably refuse to execute your first order until you have been checked out.

Having checked each other out, the next move is to establish some guidelines with your broker. This is a key step, but overlooked by most investors, sometimes with costly consequences.

## AVOIDING BROKER PROBLEMS

There is an incredible tradition of honesty and fair play that has prevailed over the years in dealings between brokers and clients.

In an age when almost every transaction requires a signature, certified cheque or cash, the informal broker-client telephone call is an almost unbelievable way of doing business. Nearly all the millions of dollars in security trading done daily is at least started by a telephone call.

But to you, as admirable as this trusting approach may be, it's worth less than yesterday's sports scores if you suddenly find that your broker has misunderstood, mismanaged or misled you about your account. And it does happen.

The odds on your ending up with a dishonest person out of the thousands of licensed securities brokers and dealers are very slim. But the mishandling of your account or a serious misunderstanding is a possibility, especially in a system so dependent on telephone conversations. You will likely never have to sue your broker for messing up your account, but knowing how to handle a misunderstanding with your broker is extremely important.

If you aren't happy with what your broker is doing or not doing, your first move should be to contact the firm involved. In almost all brokerage houses, sales staff are under the supervision of a manager who oversees transactions and the handling of portfolios. Such a person, or an officer of the firm, should be asked to look into your complaint. In almost all cases this is where the complaint stops. In most cases the firm will be inclined to take your word on what happened and the chances of your getting a settlement without much difficulty are good.

If your claim is not satisfied by the broker, your next step should be to contact the Investment Dealers Association of Canada and the major stock exchange where the transaction took place. Both the I.D.A., whose membership consists of investment houses, and the stock exchanges, have considerable regulatory and disciplinary powers over member firms — including the right to issue fines and to suspend or expel individuals or firms.

Upon receipt of your complaint, which you should submit in writing, these bodies will conduct an investigation. If they find in your favour, the broker will be under considerable pressure to settle with you quickly, particularly since disciplinary action may be taken against the individual or the firm.

If you are still not satisfied, contact the appropriate provincial securities commission. These commissions are charged with regulation of the underwriting, distribution and sale of securities, based on policies that are fairly uniform across Canada. Under the authority of the provincial Attorneys-General, securities commissions can undertake prosecutions for violations of security regulations. Bear in mind that the commissions have no power to compel a firm to return your money; they can, however, suspend a firm's registration or impose severe penalties for misrepresentation, fraud or intentional omission of material facts concerning a stock.

At this level it's important to remember that an investigation begins with your written statement of facts, which should be signed and include all relevant facts, such as the date of the transaction, details of the security involved and its price, as well as any special circumstances about the transaction. Try to recall as accurately as you can all communications you had with the broker and the date and the approximate time any telephone calls were made. List the names of all individuals in the brokerage firm you had contact with both during and after the transaction in question. If you have any record of the deal — including scribbled notes — attach copies of them to your letter. This way your complaint will have the effect of a written affidavit.

Usually, a commission will begin investigating on an informal basis, sending its investigators to interview you, the broker and any others involved. If a formal investigation is called for, the commission can subpoena records and witnesses.

After the investigation of your complaint by the security commission, a hearing, which could last anywhere from a couple of hours to days, depending on the complexity of the matter, may be held. At its conclusion, the broker, if found to be at fault, may be reprimanded, suspended or expelled from the securities industry. But, if not, and you are determined to pursue the case, your next recourse would be to file a civil suit. Time to get a lawyer.

On a simple complaint — say a disagreement between you and your salesman over the number of shares purchased in your name — the investigation would probably take a few days. More complex cases involving possible fraud or misrepresentation could take months.

The most frequent complaints concern simple misunderstandings, but they often pose the toughest problems for investigators. If, say, you asked your broker to buy 100 shares of a stock and he purchased 500, the only evidence is your word against his, and you often can't do much about the complaint. Of course, if it happens with more than one client, then the broker's credibility begins to suffer.

Legally, your oral order to a broker constitutes an enforceable contract. The only exception involves purchase of new stock by prospectus when you can withdraw an order within 48 hours after receipt of the prospectus. Though binding, the contract is, of course, subject to proof. In a dispute based on a telephone call, proof will likely depend on the relative credibility of the witnesses — you and the broker, that is.

Even in a case where your broker is disputing what you said, you will probably win if you have taken the trouble to jot down a few notes detailing the telephone call at the time. While not evidence in the strictest sense of the word, a memo including the date, time and details of the order would lend support to your recollection of an oral order. People can pretty well judge the veracity of an individual, and if you've got a memo or notes confirming your side of the story you will likely be in the driver's seat.

Your other alternative following a dispute is simply not to pay. If you have a genuine grievance, brokerage firms will rarely resort to a court proceeding in order to collect your account. The cost to the firm in time, expense and public relations is usually prohibitive. If, however, the value of the stock in question has dropped following your disputed purchase, be prepared. A firm may decide to sell the stock and sue you for the difference between the original purchase price and their loss. In most cases involving small amounts, the firm will write off the loss — and you as well.

The market is full of habitual complainers and if your refusal to pay is really based on sour grapes after taking a loss, don't expect to get away with it. The brokerage industry is well aware that the world is full of people on both sides who might be stretching facts a bit to get things to work out in their favour. If you make a practice of not paying losses, you could end up blacklisted. Though no actual list is said to exist, the industry does take steps to protect itself from chronic offenders. It is rumoured the Toronto Stock Exchange occasionally sends member houses names of people who may have had questionable dealings with a member firm. Other firms which have had dealings with the individual are asked to contact the exchange. Such notices, said to appear on average about once a month, are posted in the order and clearance departments of member houses.

So checks and balances do exist on both sides to weed out brokers and investors who don't belong in the securities field. Like most grievance procedures, however, those existing for the benefit of the investor are best if they are never needed. One way to avoid disputes is to clarify the ground rules your broker acts under and to review them every now and then. Let him or her know that you are aware of your rights. Above all, keep your broker informed about your financial circumstances and investment objectives.

When initiating a transaction, be sure your broker completely understands your order. Take the time to question any strange terms he may use when he reads your order back on the telephone. Your best defense is knowledge. There is no way you can let someone else blindly run your financial affairs for you. It you're interested in shares of companies in a particular industry, you should learn as much as you can about four or five companies in that or similar industries. Take the trouble to obtain the annual reports and read them. See what the market price movements of the particular companies have been. Without this research, you will wind up trying to evaluate the broker instead of the stocks.

However you arrange your dealings with your broker, remember that reliability does not automatically mean profit. If you intend to play the market you will have to take risks that should be made on the basis of *your knowledge*, not your broker's opinion. Finally, bear in mind the next time you call your broker just how imperfect the telephone alone is as a communications link. Make notes — and keep them. Your broker probably does.

## Do's and Don'ts

Here are some basic ways to reduce the risk of misunderstanding between you and your broker.

### Do's

1. Deal only with securities houses which meet the standards of the Investment Dealers Association or one of the major stock exchanges. Select a dealer or broker who operates an office near you, has a sales representative with whom you are able to establish a close working relationship and one who provides the type of services you are especially interested in (e.g. research, new issue underwriting, mutual funds, etc.).
2. Require, as part of the terms for opening a discretionary account, that you receive from the broker on a regular basis a written report of the status of your account.

**3.** Tell your broker when you are most reachable. Your broker should know whether you prefer to be called at the office. If there is a number where you can always be reached, you should consider giving it to your broker.

**4.** Make decisions — whether yes or no. Always hesitating to act on recommendations will work against you. Your broker probably has hundreds of clients to service; if you always hedge you're very apt to be put at the end of the list.

**5.** Be cautious about which firm and individual you decide to deal with.

### Don'ts

**1.** Don't deal in securities sold under high pressure whether in the form of a telephone call or letter. Request the person offering securities to mail you written information about the company, its operations, net profit, management, financial position and future prospects. If you do not understand the written information, consult someone who does.

**2.** Don't deal with a person who guarantees what the price of a stock is going to be in the future or offers to buy it back from you at cost if it doesn't go up in value.

**3.** Don't deal with a representative of a securities firm which is unknown to you until you have had time to carefully check the company's reputation.

**4.** Don't invest on rumours. So-called inside information is quickly discounted by the market — usually long before you hear it. This probably is the basis for the adage "sell on good news, buy on bad news."

## SOURCES OF INFORMATION

It seems ridiculous to have to say it, but many people who consider themselves to be competent investors totally ignore the main ingredient required in order to make sensible investment decisions: information.

If you obtain as much information as you possibly can about a company before committing funds to the purchase of its securities, you will be considerably more secure in your choices than those who blindly plunge in and take a chance.

**FIGURE 4 Partial List of Stock Market Quotations for Shares Listed on the Toronto Stock Exchange from Globe and Mail Report on Business.**

Date of transactions

Lowest price paid that day

Highest price paid that day

Last price that day

Stock Exchange

Warrants

Total number of shares traded that day

**QUOTATIONS FOR AUGUST 18, 1983, PREPARED BY THE TORONTO STOCK EXCHANGE**

| 1983 High | 1983 Low | Stock | Div | Days High | Days Low | Days Close | Ch'ge | Vol |
|---|---|---|---|---|---|---|---|---|
| 13 | 6 5/8 | A.G.F.M | .56 | $11 5/8 | 11 1/2 | 11 1/2 | - 1/8 | 400 |
| 30 3/4 | 18 3/4 | AMCA Int | a1.00 | $26 1/4 | 26 | 26 1/4 | + 1/4 | 19500 |
| 25 3/4 | 18 | Abti Prce | .80 | $24 1/2 | 24 | 24 | | 639 |
| 50 1/2 | 44 | Abitbi 10 | 5.00 | $47 1/2 | 47 1/2 | 47 1/2 | - 1/2 | 150 |
| 90 | 53 | Adanac M o | | 60 | 60 | 60 | - 2 | 1500 |
| 230 | 155 | Agassiz o | | 212 | 210 | 212 | + 2 | 3350 |
| 21 | 14 1/8 | Agnico E | a .05 | $20 3/8 | 20 | 20 1/4 | | 15900 |
| 6 7/8 | 485 | Agra Ind A | .10 | $6 1/2 | 6 1/8 | 6 1/8 | - 3/8 | 2800 |
| 5 3/4 | 450 | Agra B f | .10 | $5 3/4 | 5 5/8 | 5 3/4 | + 1/8 | 2400 |
| 14 1/4 | 8 | Aiguebel o | | $13 | 12 5/8 | 12 5/8 | - 3/8 | 1350 |
| 163 | 101 | Albany o | | 140 | 140 | 140 | | 1000 |
| 20 3/4 | 13 5/8 | Alt Energy | .20 | $19 1/2 | 19 1/4 | 19 1/4 | - 1/8 | 72485 |
| 33 1/2 | 29 1/2 | Alt Enr A | 3.75 | $30 1/4 | 30 | 30 1/4 | - 1/8 | 2300 |
| 29 | 22 1/2 | Alta Nat | 1.32 | $25 3/4 | 25 3/4 | 25 3/4 | + 1/4 | 200 |
| 47 1/8 | 32 1/8 | Alcan | a .90 | $47 | 46 1/4 | 46 5/8 | + 1/8 | 167295 |
| 18 3/8 | 7 3/8 | Alcan w | | $18 3/8 | 17 5/8 | 18 | | 87110 |
| 37 5/8 | 24 3/4 | Algoma St | | $31 7/8 | 31 3/4 | 31 3/4 | + 1/4 | 6926 |
| 105 | 50 | Altex o | | 70 | 70 | 70 | | 5000 |
| 27 | 22 3/4 | Alum A | 2.31 | $25 3/4 | 25 1/4 | 25 5/8 | + 1/4 | 24500 |
| 26 1/8 | 22 | Alum 1st p | 2.00 | $25 | 25 | 25 | | 100 |
| 261 | 140 | Am Eagle o | | 250 | 246 | 246 | | 14770 |
| 53 | 26 | Am Leduc | | 31 | 31 | 31 | - 1 | 1000 |
| 29 | 21 | Andrs WA f | .96 5/8 | $28 | 28 | 28 | | 310 |
| 65 | 35 | Anthes | | 52 | 52 | 52 | - 3 | 10000 |
| 8 | 475 | Argus C pr | | $7 1/2 | 7 1/2 | 7 1/2 | - 1/4 | 1167 |
| 300 | 155 | Argyll E A | | 260 | 255 | 255 | - 5 | 2150 |
| 300 | 210 | Argyll E B | | 280 | 280 | 280 | | 150 |
| 365 | 195 | Argyll o | | 275 | 275 | 275 | - 10 | 1125 |
| 53 | 16 1/4 | Asamera | .40 | $48 1/2 | 45 7/8 | 47 5/8 | + 1 3/8 | 57800 |
| 14 | 9 1/2 | Asbestos | | $11 7/8 | 11 3/4 | 11 7/8 | + 1/8 | 1037 |
| 8 1/8 | 375 | Asoc Porc o | | 385 | 385 | 385 | | 1500 |
| 10 | 430 | Astral f | .15 | $7 3/4 | 7 3/4 | 7 3/4 | + 1/8 | 300 |
| 11 1/2 | 8 1/2 | Atco I f | .20 | $9 1/8 | 8 7/8 | 8 7/8 | - 1/4 | 3396 |
| 11 1/4 | 8 3/8 | Atco II | .20 | $9 | 8 3/4 | 9 | + 1/4 | 500 |
| 35 | 30 | Atco 11 1/2 | 2.87 | $33 3/8 | 33 | 33 3/8 | + 1/8 | 1200 |
| 115 | 61 | Atlantis o | | 109 | 105 | 105 | + 1 | 23800 |
| 54 | 30 1/2 | Atlas Yk o | | 47 | 45 | 47 | - 1 | 6500 |
| 315 | 140 | Augmitto o | | 190 | 181 | 183 | - 1 | 7650 |
| 25 | 15 | Augmito w | | 25 | 23 | 25 | + 2 | 3400 |
| 117 | | Aur Res o | | 117 | 113 | 115 | - 2 | 10000 |
| 12 | 7 1/2 | Ato Hard A | | $11 1/2 | 11 1/4 | 11 1/4 | | 500 |

| 1983 High | 1983 Low | Stock | Div | Days High | Days Low | Days Close | Ch'ge | Vol |
|---|---|---|---|---|---|---|---|---|
| 14 1/8 | 6 1/8 | Dofasco wt | | $12 7/8 | 12 7/8 | 12 7/8 | - 3/8 | 480 |
| 10 3/4 | 460 | Doman A | | $9 5/8 | 9 3/8 | 9 3/8 | - 1/8 | 4644 |
| 6 5/8 | 405 | Dome Cda | | $6 | 5 7/8 | 5 7/8 | | 19624 |
| 39 | 2 | Dme Cda w | | 5 | 3 1/2 | 4 | + 2 | 78980 |
| 27 1/4 | 17 7/8 | Dome Mine | .12 | $22 1/2 | 22 | 22 | - 1/4 | 88052 |
| 7 | 310 | Dome Pete | | $6 | 5 5/8 | 5 3/4 | + 1/8 | 223170 |
| 16 | 12 1/4 | DPete A p | 1.94 | $14 | 13 7/8 | 14 | | 4600 |
| 15 3/4 | 12 1/8 | DPete B p | y1.94 | $13 5/8 | 13 5/8 | 13 5/8 | | 237 |
| 20 | 8 | D Pete w | | 11 | 10 | 10 | | 90029 |
| 170 | 85 | D Explor o | | 94 | 92 | 92 | - 6 | 4100 |
| 20 1/2 | 15 1/2 | Dom Store | 1.00 | $19 1/2 | 19 1/4 | 19 1/4 | - 1/4 | 17460 |
| 20 1/2 | 13 1/4 | D Textie | .72 | $19 1/4 | 19 1/8 | 19 1/4 | | 1200 |
| 27 3/4 | 19 5/8 | Domtar | 1.00 | $26 3/8 | 26 1/4 | 26 1/4 | - 1/4 | 1815 |
| 50 | 25 | Dorset o | | 39 1/2 | 36 | 37 | + 2 | 12500 |
| 95 | 34 | Drm Pete o | | 83 | 80 | 80 | - 2 | 46850 |
| 160 | 50 | Dunraine o | | 115 | 115 | 115 | - 5 | 8550 |
| 31 1/8 | 17 | Du Pont A | .24 | $31 | 31 | 31 | | 12100 |
| 29 3/4 | 10 | Dylex Ltd | .36 | $26 3/4 | 26 3/4 | 26 3/4 | - 1/4 | 200 |
| 22 1/8 | 10 5/8 | Dylex A f | .36 | $19 3/4 | 19 1/2 | 19 3/4 | + 1/4 | 4000 |
| 260 | 140 | Dynamar | | 174 | 170 | 174 | + 3 | 6700 |
| 12 | 8 3/4 | Dynmr 105 | 1.05 | $11 3/8 | 11 1/4 | 11 1/4 | | 950 |
| 145 | 65 | Dynex A | | 80 | 78 | 80 | | 2000 |
| 450 | 270 | Eaglet o | | 320 | 315 | 320 | + 5 | 2400 |
| 10 | 8 3/8 | Eaton A | 1.07 | $9 1/4 | 9 1/4 | 9 1/4 | + 1/8 | 100 |
| 12 3/8 | 7 1/4 | Echo Bay | .08 3/8 | $12 3/8 | 11 5/8 | 11 3/4 | - 1/8 | 50340 |
| 27 | 20 3/4 | Echo B 300 | 3.00 | $24 5/8 | 24 3/8 | 24 1/2 | - 1/4 | 4172 |
| 7 3/4 | 5 | Echo 1986 w | | $6 1/4 | 6 1/8 | 6 1/4 | + 1/8 | 750 |
| 7 5/8 | 475 | Echo 1987 w | | $5 3/4 | 5 5/8 | 5 3/4 | + 1/4 | 1800 |
| 7 5/8 | 465 | Echo 1988 w | | $6 | 5 1/2 | 6 | + 1/2 | 6700 |
| 7 5/8 | 470 | Echo 1989 w | | $6 | 5 7/8 | 6 | + 1/8 | 3100 |
| 95 | 50 | Ego Res o | | 52 | 51 | 52 | + 1 | 8600 |
| 9 1/4 | 6 3/8 | Elcthom X | .10 | $7 1/2 | 7 1/2 | 7 1/2 | | 700 |
| 9 3/8 | 6 | Elcthm Y f | .11 | $7 3/8 | 7 3/8 | 7 3/8 | - 1/8 | 650 |
| 350 | 165 | Elks | | 220 | 190 | 210 | - 10 | 11000 |
| 16 1/2 | 9 7/8 | Empire A f | .64 | $16 | 16 | 16 | | 100 |
| 185 | 72 | Energy R o | | 130 | 130 | 130 | + 10 | 5450 |
| 245 | 115 | Epitek | | 120 | 118 | 120 | + 2 | 6250 |
| 19 | 11 3/8 | Equity Svr | | $16 7/8 | 16 5/8 | 16 5/8 | + 1/4 | 2960 |
| 18 1/2 | 10 1/4 | Extendcar | .30 | $18 1/2 | 17 3/4 | 18 1/8 | + 1 | 7293 |
| 18 1/2 | 10 1/8 | Extndcr A f | .40 | $18 1/2 | 17 3/4 | 18 1/4 | + 1/2 | 5614 |
| 19 7/8 | 12 1/2 | FCA Intl | .16 | $18 1/2 | 18 1/4 | 18 1/4 | + 1/4 | 700 |

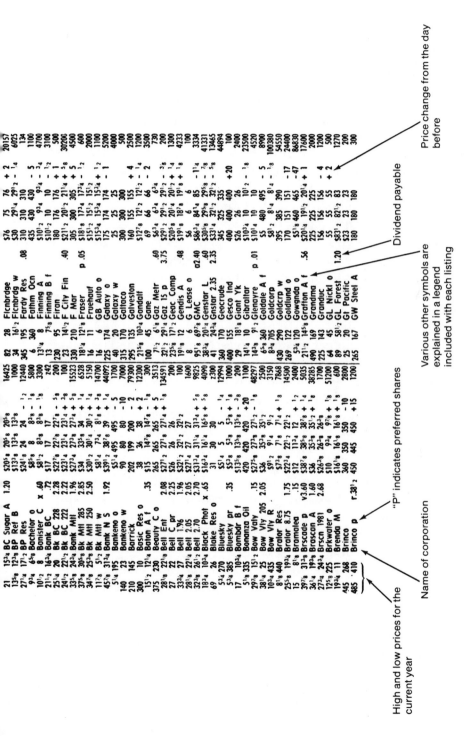

Price change from the day before

Dividend payable

Various other symbols are explained in a legend included with each listing

"P" indicates preferred shares

Name of corporation

High and low prices for the current year

There is lots of information available. Canadian securities legislation is based on the principle of full and true disclosure of information pertaining to issuers of securities, and annual and interim financial reports of those who are subject to their rules. In addition, Canada is blessed with a fine financial press, not to mention the many American publications available.

There are really three routes available. The first is to rely entirely on investment counsellors or brokers. If you have neither the time nor the inclination to do your own investigations, this is the way to go. The second method is to be your own researcher. The third route, and probably the most satisfying — and perhaps the best — is a combination of the first two.

The Canadian business and financial press is varied and informative. It ranges from daily newspaper financial pages and sections, through weekly business newspapers to monthly business magazines. (A sample of stock market listings is shown in figure 4.) Examples are *The Globe and Mail Report on Business, Financial Times of Canada, Financial Post, Canadian Business* and *Executive Magazine.*

In addition, many Canadian investment houses and the major Canadian financial institutions issue regular reports dealing with current business, economic and political trends, and items of general interest. Look for them at your bank and trust company branch. The investment houses also frequently publish special industry and company reports.

As you would expect, there are numerous U.S. financial publications which are of interest to Canadian investors. Two truly outstanding American financial publications are the daily *Wall Street Journal* and the weekly *Barrons.* Some of the more relevant American financial magazines are *Money, Fortune, Forbes, Commercial and Financial Chronicle, Investment Dealer's Digest* and *The Institutional Investor.*

For those who want to delve even deeper into financial and business information, there are many Canadian government publications available.

*Weekly Financial Statistics*: This one covers the volume and yields of treasury bills sold at the government's weekly auction and a report on government security yields — none of which is of too much interest to the individual investor. But it also includes information on total government direct and guaranteed debt outstanding as well as balances of the Bank of Canada and the chartered banks.

*Monthly Review*: A wealth of statistical information including federal, provincial and municipal debt outstanding; security yields and retirements; retail sales; price indexes; and stock market indexes.

*Bank of Canada Annual Report*: This voluminous publication sums up the year's economic highlights and contains much interesting data in chart and graph form. Although some of it is very technical, there is also much of interest to the less experienced investor as well.

*Statistics Canada*: There's almost no end to the information — useful and useless — which is available from this source. Its data gathering and publishing is a whole industry unto itself, from which you can obtain information on the trends and activity in practically any industry in Canada — whether they're expanding, orders placed, retail sales, manufacturing activity, inventory levels, bankruptcies, and on and on.

*The Canadian Statistical Review*: Another Statistics Canada publication. This is a monthly summary of current Canadian economic indicators as well as historical data.

Last, but certainly not least, the Toronto, Montreal and Vancouver stock exchanges publish excellent monthly bulletins (available at very little cost) outlining information about the Canadian securities markets.

# chapter nineteen

# *Common Shares*

## WHAT ARE COMMON SHARES?

The common shares of public companies are by far the most popular investment vehicle among people who play the market. It seems incredible, then, that many investors are completely unaware that a common share is anything other than a thing which they bought and hope to sell sometime in the future at a profit. It is much more than that.

First and foremost, common shares represent the residual ownership of an incorporated business. After creditors are paid and preferred shares redeemed, the common shareholders are entitled to all the remaining assets of the corporation regardless of the par value or actual cost of the common share.

Moreover, common shares are normally voting shares. Indeed, it is a rare set of circumstances in which the common shareholders do not have voting control of a corporation. Ownership of even one common share will normally entitle you to a vote at the shareholders' meetings.

In addition, many common share issues pay regular dividends, thereby forming an integral part of many investors' income package. And of course, the common share is the investment looked to by most investors for capital growth.

Common share ownership is usually evidenced by registered, transferable, engraved printed sheets called share certificates. This is the actual legal document giving legal ownership of the shares described on it. The reason for engraving share certificates on high grade paper is to make forgery of them more difficult.

If you are the registered owner of common shares — meaning that your name is in the share register of the corporation as the holder of the particular certificates — your name will appear on the share certificate along with the number of shares that certificate represents. On the other hand, certificates are often in "street" form. A street certificate is made out in the name of an investment dealer or stockholder and endorsed by that company or person on the back. This means the shares are freely negotiable and acceptable for delivery anywhere in the country. They change hands many times with no actual change in registration being made in the corporation's share register.

If you are merely trading in common shares to make gains, it's of little concern whether the certificates are in street form or not. However, if you intend to hold dividend-paying shares for a long time, or want to receive directly company annual reports, etc., you should have the shares registered in *your* name, or in the name of a nominee, because all dividend cheques, reports and other shareholder data are sent to the registered owner, which is the name appearing on the certificate. But, of course, whether your certificates are being held in street or registered form, you'll want to be sure they're kept in a safe place to avoid theft or forgery. Most investors keep their securities either in a safety deposit box or held in safekeeping by their brokers, bank or trust company. They should not be left lying around the house or work place. This is particularly so if the certificates are in street form, in which case only theft is necessary for you to suffer a loss. Certificates in street form are perfectly negotiable with no need to forge anything on them.

If you own a dividend-paying stock in street form, the dividends will be paid to the dealer or broker whose name appears on the certificate. You need only get in touch with the dealer or broker concerned in order to collect your dividend. Indeed, in most cases the broker will automatically send you a cheque. Usually, the dealer or broker will issue the information slip reporting interest and dividend income for tax purposes to you showing the amount and type of income received on your behalf.

## Dividends

It must always be remembered that the payment of dividends on common shares is not automatic. The board of directors must first decide whether a dividend will be paid at all. Then they decide the amount and when the actual payment will be made. Payments may be quarterly, semi-annual, annual, or follow no fixed pattern at all. Special dividends are sometimes declared.

If shareholders are not happy with the board's dividend policy — or lack thereof — their options are to sell the shares or vote against re-election of the recalcitrant directors.

### Ex-Dividend; Cum-Dividend

When a corporation has a lot of shareholders it usually advertises the declaration of a dividend in the financial press. There are two key dates attached to a dividend declaration. The first is the date "of record." The second is the payment date.

When a stock is actively traded, the record of shareholders' names is constantly changing. Therefore, the corporation must pick a time at which the shareholders who are to receive the dividend are determined. The shareholders whose names appear on the corporation's records as of that date will receive the dividend.

The usual pattern is to name a record date a week or two subsequent to the date the dividend is declared. For example, a corporation might declare a dividend on May 25th payable to shareholders of record as of the close of business on June 8th. The record date would be June 8th.

The payment date of the dividend would be two weeks to a month later — to allow time for the preparation of cheques. In this case, the payment date might be June 29th.

You can readily see there will be some shareholders whose purchases and sales will straddle these dates. In order to determine whether it is the buyer or seller who is entitled to the dividend, the stock exchange will name an "ex-dividend date." On and after this date, the shares are sold "ex-dividend," which means the seller retains the right to the dividend and the buyer will not get it. The ex-dividend date is usually four business days before the dividend record date. In the above example, then, anyone buying the stock on or after June 4th would likely *not* receive the dividend. This fact will be reflected in the price paid for the shares.

"Cum-dividend" is, of course, the reverse. Purchasers of the stock in our example between May 25th and June 4th would know they'll be receiving the dividend — not the seller —and will pay a correspondingly higher price for the shares.

## Stock Dividends

Sometimes dividends are paid in the form of additional shares rather than in cash. This is called a stock dividend. Corporations will sometimes do this when they have sufficient earnings to warrant a dividend payment but want to preserve cash, say, for expansion.

Theoretically, the recipient of a stock dividend can turn it into cash by selling his or her "new" shares.

## Regular and Extra Dividends

Many public corporations that pay common share dividends designate a specified amount which will be paid each year in the absence of evil times befalling the corporation. Such dividends are usually called "regular" dividends. In some cases these corporations then pay an additional dividend at the end of the fiscal year. The financial press usually refers to these payments as "extra" dividends. The term "extra" is a precaution to investors and potential investors that they should not assume the extra dividend will be paid the following year.

It is usual to include extra dividends in the calculation of yield for common stock. However, if in doubt, the conservative approach is to calculate the yield based on regular dividends only. In any event, when reading the financial press, always check the legend and symbols to determine whether the indicated dividend is regular or extra. If it isn't stated clearly, a further inquiry is in order before making an investment in the expectation of a repeated dividend when the corporation may have no intention of continuing it.

## Dividend Re-investment Plans

Some public companies have introduced an option for shareholders called a dividend re-investment plan. For the shareholders who so elect, the corporation, instead of paying cash dividends to the shareholders, uses the funds to purchase additional shares of its own stock on behalf of the shareholder, which in effect turns the dividend into a stock dividend. In most cases these purchases are made on the open market by a trustee who periodically keeps the shareholders informed of their status under the plan.

The advantage to the shareholders of dividend re-investment plans is the provision of an automatic savings plan allowing them to re-invest small amounts of cash in shares in circumstances under which they could not otherwise do so, because individually the amounts would be too small to purchase full shares and fractions of shares can't be bought in the market. By combining their dividends, though, the shareholders make sufficient funds available to the trustees to buy in bulk, thereby realizing considerable savings on commissions in comparison to what the individual shareholders would have to pay to buy odd lots — if, indeed they could. Furthermore, there is no difficulty in the trustees allocating fractions of shares to participants.

Some corporations have plans permitting participants to contribute cash to the plans which in turn is used by the trustee to purchase shares. Again, the attraction is economy of scale. Limits, such as $1,000 per quarter, are usually placed on the amounts of cash that can be contributed.

## Splits

When a corporation's earnings grow and dividends increase, the market price of its shares rises considerably. The higher the price of shares, the more restricted their marketability becomes because small investors can't afford to buy a lot of highly priced stock, and bigger investors are sometimes loathe to put all their eggs in one basket.

There are a number of reasons why corporations like to have a wide distribution of their shares. The more shareholders a company has, the easier it is to raise additional capital through the sale of new securities. Also, employees who own shares tend to be more highly motivated than those who do not. And, not to be overlooked is the simple fact that shareholders are more likely to buy the corporation's products or use its services. Accordingly, when the directors of a corporation feel the high price of their shares is inhibiting wide distribution, they "split" the shares. This is accomplished by submitting to a shareholders' vote a by-law permitting a subdivision of the shares. This can be done at the annual meeting, or at a special general meeting called for that particular purpose.

Once shareholder approval is obtained, the actual share split is strictly a mechanical procedure that does not change the actual capital of the corporation. For example, shares with a market value of $100 might be split five for one resulting in the market value dropping to $20 per share. The existing shareholders are in exactly the same position as before the split, except they now have five shares worth $20 each instead of one share worth $100.

The logistics are as follows. In the case of stated par value shares, the old share certificates are called in and new ones issued for the larger number of shares. In the case of no par value stock, an announcement is made in the financial press (and, obviously, directly to the existing shareholders), and certificates for the additional shares created by the split are mailed out to the shareholders.

There are no income tax implications to a share split and there is no reason why a shareholder should resist a split because the total value of his holdings remains the same as does his pro rata interest in the corporation.

## Reverse Splits

We have just described the mechanics and effect of a stock split. The reverse situation, sometimes called a consolidation, occurs occasionally.

The mechanics are similar to a stock split but the result, of course, is the opposite. On a consolidation, for example, four shares worth 25 cents each might be replaced with one share worth one dollar. As in the case of splits, the shareholder's total investment and pro rata interest in the company remain the same, there is no change in the corporation's capitalization, and there is no income tax effect.

Reverse splits usually take place in low-priced junior mining and oil and gas exploration companies. A reverse split raises the market price of the shares and places the corporation (mainly because of investor psychology) in a better position to raise additional capital through the sale of new shares.

## Rights

A "right" is the term given to the privilege granted by a corporation to its existing shareholders to acquire additional shares directly from the corporation itself. This is simply a method of raising additional capital for the corporation while allowing the existing shareholders to avoid dilution of their shareholdings without the necessity of incurring commission expenses or the additional cost resulting from an increase in market prices caused by new demands for stock. As a matter of fact, the offering price for the new shares is normally a bit lower than the current market price of the old shares with the result that the rights themselves have a value.

The privilege attached to the rights is in direct proportion to the number of shares already owned. For example, the "right" may be the opportunity to purchase one share for each ten shares owned. As mentioned, the price of the one new share would likely be a bit less than the current market value.

Because the rights themselves have a value, a market for them usually develops quickly, allowing any shareholders who do not want to exercise their rights to make some money by selling them. Obviously, additional rights can be purchased by existing share-holders, and non-shareholders can get into the act by acquiring rights on the open market. If the corporation issuing the rights is listed on a stock exchange, the rights themselves will automatically be listed when the usual red tape has been cleared away.

Remember that rights normally have a very short life. They usually have to be exercised within a month or so, after which they expire and become worthless.

The logistics of a rights issue are identical to the payment of a dividend. The corporation's shareholders book of record is closed as of the close of business on a particular date and shareholders of record at that time receive rights in the form of certificates.

As in the case of dividends, shares go "ex-rights" four business days before the record date. Purchasers of shares after the ex-rights date will not be entitled to the relevant rights — that privilege stays with the seller. Between the time of the announcement that rights will be issued and the ex-rights date the shares are described as "cum rights" and the purchaser will be entitled to receive the rights.

Although they are usually transferable it is completely within a corporation's power to issue rights which can be exercised only by existing shareholders. But this is rare.

A non-shareholder buying transferable rights on the open market is able to exercise them under the same conditions as the original rights holder.

The price of rights tends to rise and fall as the price of the relevant common stock rises and falls, but not always in lock-step. Their theoretical value is affected by buying and selling costs and the ever-present influences of supply and demand.

## Warrants

Rights and warrants are not exactly the same things, although they do have some similarities.

A warrant, like a right, is really an option to buy capital stock and is traded on the stock market. However, in contrast to a right which usually has a very limited life, warrants often have terms extending for years. And, whereas rights are initially issued to existing shareholders before finding their way into the market-place, warrants are often attached to bond, debenture and pre-ferred share issues. They are detachable (either immediately or after a relatively short period of time) and then trade on their own.

The main attraction of both rights and warrants is that they permit investment in the issuing company at considerably lower levels of absolute dollars than investing in the actual shares. It follows that this limits potential losses and a conservative investor might prefer the rights or warrants route in an uncertain situation.

## Income Tax

The income tax treatment of investment income and capital gains and losses is constantly being changed by the government. You should keep up-to-date on the current law by, as recommended earlier, obtaining the readily available, and easily readable, summaries provided free by most firms of chartered accountants and most financial institutions, such as banks, trust companies and insurance companies.

# FACTORS AFFECTING COMMON SHARE PRICES

Now, let's turn to some of the factors affecting common share prices. Actually, common share prices are probably the best example of a free market operation because they rise and fall in direct response to supply and demand. It is necessary, then, to understand what determines the demand level.

Any such analysis runs the risk of being over-simplified because the subject is tremendously complex. But, there are five fundamental forces which probably yield the greatest influence and these are easily understood. They are:

1. profit and dividend outlook,
2. investors' resources,
3. tax outlook,
4. economic outlook, and
5. technical market factors.

Each deserves examination in greater detail.

### Profit and Dividend Outlook

This market force itself has a number of facets, any one of which can significantly affect the market price of common shares. For example, consider the effect on the stock market of the federal government's announcement in October 1975, that the anti-inflation rules to be introduced would include restrictions on payment of dividends. Right after the announcement the general price level of common stocks on Canadian stock exchanges declined.

Conversely, two years later, when the federal government announced that controls would be phased out, there followed a general rise in stock prices which had to be due, at least in part, to that particular announcement. But these circumstances were unusual in that they affected the market outlook as a whole. Usually, the profit and dividend outlook is considered in the context of a particular stock.

One facet of this outlook that will drive up a stock's price, as has been witnessed many times in the past, is the possibility of a takeover bid, merger or other such major development. Although you might think a crystal ball is necessary to ferret out these situations, this is really not the case. Experienced investment analysts can often identify public companies that are ripe for a takeover.

The most usual consideration which investors rely on, though, is the company's earnings outlook. In short, an informed guess as to when and to what degree a company is going to have a significant improvement in its earnings or dividend pay-outs — or both.

This type of prediction has to be made in the light of three interrelated factors: the economy; the industry; and, the particular company itself.

More important, the prediction has to be made and acted upon before the majority of other investors reach the same conclusion. Otherwise, the expected favourable conditions will already be reflected in the market price of the stock. This is what is meant by the expression "already discounted by the market."

The price-earnings ratio and yield of a particular stock, in relation to other stocks in similar circumstances, are two rules-of-thumb by which an investor can tell whether the market price is high or low in relation to anticipated company earnings. For example, assume two companies in the same industry — say company A and B — seem to be equally sound financially and both well managed. If company A's price-earnings ratio is higher than company B's, then company B's stock might be a better buy in terms of future growth. Similarly, if the yield on company B's stock (the dividend divided by your cost per share) is higher than company A's, you'll get a better return on your money by investing in company B. Either of these situations suggest that company B's market price might be low or company A's high. But, be sure there isn't some other reason for the difference. The easiest way to find out is to ask your broker for an explanation.

### Investors' Resources

An obvious factor affecting the demand for common shares — or any investment for that matter — is the amount of money that the general investing public has to invest. This includes the funds that find their way into common stocks through financial institutions such as mutual funds, trust companies and insurance companies.

The more discretionary income there is available, the more demand there is apt to be for common shares. For example, a general income tax cut should have a positive general effect on stock prices.

This leads naturally into the next fundamental factor.

## Tax Outlook

Many income tax regulations have a direct effect on stock prices. The sweetening of the dividend tax credit in the mid-70s made investment in the stock market a more attractive option and consequently caused an increase in stock prices. An announcement of an intention to eliminate the capital gains tax on common shares would undoubtedly increase demand, and, therefore, prices.

In a nutshell, tax increases, either at the corporation or shareholder level, tend to lower stock prices while tax decreases at either level tend to increase stock prices.

It is apparent, then, that a budget speech is an event which might well have a profound effect on stock prices. Who can forget the devastating effect on the prices of natural resource stocks when the federal and provincial governments almost taxed them out of existence in the early 70s?

## Economic Outlook

When people think the economy will be in good shape in the foreseeable future, they invest more in common stocks in order to share in the expected economic growth. If the past is any indication, this will result in an increase in value of publicly-traded common shares. On the other hand, during times of economic pessimism, investors have a tendency to put their money in high-yield debt securities, high-quality preferreds, or just leave it in savings accounts or short-term paper — all to the detriment of the demand for common shares with the predictable bad effect on their general price level.

The general economic outlook can actually have more far-reaching effects, which in turn affect the demand for common share investments. Quite apart from and in addition to the direct effect just described, the general economic outlook also influences the overall demand by corporations and all levels of government for capital as well as the actual supply of capital that is available for all types of investments, from institutions as well as individuals. Again, in optimistic times the effect on common share prices is positive; in times of pessimism the effect is bad.

Some of the barometers which sophisticated investors use to gauge the economic outlook are: interest rate trends; the rate of inflation; unemployment levels; wage settlements; general labour unrest; the value of the dollar; the federal government's monetary policy; general profit trends; and, the probable effects of recent or anticipated government budgets — most generally the federal budget, but astute investors are aware of the impact on stock prices a particular provincial budget provision might have. Significant changes in provincial natural resource taxation is one example that comes readily to mind. For example, if Alberta or Ontario raises its royalty charge on oil or mining operations, this would undoubtedly have an adverse effect on the shares of companies operating in those provinces, unless investors were confident the increased cost of operation could be passed on to consumers.

### Technical Market Factors

Last, but by no means least, of the five fundamental factors affecting the demand for, and therefore the price of, common shares, is what the professional investors term "technical" market factors. In plain language, the term means nothing more than the effect of investor psychology; in short, the reaction by investors to the other four fundamental factors. But, it deserves closer examination.

No informed analyst doubts the effect of investor psychology on the market prices of common shares, or any other investment for that matter. As a matter of fact, there are many analysts who believe the psychological factor is so important that they practically ignore attempts to predict future earnings for a particular stock and instead plot the stock's price performance on charts and base their price predictions on the patterns this shows. This is called in the trade a "technical" analysis, in contrast to "fundamental" analysis which is based on earnings trends. Anyone who doubts the validity of technical analysis — and there are many who do — might pause to consider the many times when a stock's price swings radically in the absence of a fundamental change in the company's earnings outlook or any other rational reason therefor.

The basic theory underlying technical analysis is that the future trend of a stock's price is predictable from its past range of prices in relation to the volume of trading. Technical analysts believe their charts allow them to predict when a heavy demand or sudden supply is imminent. To take a very simple illustration, it's likely that news of a favourable or unfavourable development which is apt to affect a company's share price tends to spread in waves from one group of investors or potential investors to another. The whole investment world doesn't hear about it, or react to it, at the same time.

If it's a favourable development, first one group of people will hear about it and will buy stock, driving its price up on a heavy volume of trading. Then there will be a lull and the stock will sell off a bit on a low and declining volume. After a while a new group of people will get the news and buy the stock, again driving up the price on heavy volume. Then another lull and so on until the effect of the news peters out. Of course, if it is an unfavourable development the effect on demand and price would be the opposite.

When a technical analyst spots this type of pattern on a chart, he or she assumes there is something going on that is affecting investor psychology and that money can be made trading that stock.

Remember, though, there are innumerable and various formations on charts which the technical analyst uses to make interpretations. It's pretty risky business. You must always remember the demand and supply factors the technicians are watching for are actually the result of one or more of the other fundamental factors translated into investor psychology. The point is, if these trends can be spotted well in advance of the crowd, it should be possible to make some money in the market.

Technical analysis is, therefore, an additional tool which might assist in fine-tuning the timing of purchases and sales. There's little doubt it is helpful to consider the potential demand for a stock in addition to the fundamental earnings picture. In this context facts are important only in respect to what people think about them.

Investors in common shares must always remember that the main characteristics distinguishing common shares from bonds or preferred shares is their tendency to be subject to wide price swings. For example, in any twelve month period wide price ranges are apt to be experienced by even traditional highly regarded common shares. Watch IBM for example.

It's trite to say that anyone who can predict such swings with accuracy will be able to make a great deal of money. Of course, that is impossible to do. But, the other end of the stick is to blindly buy and sell, strictly on instinct (or lack thereof), without giving consideration to the major factors which affect share prices. These were dealt with above, but some underlying aspects of these factors are always particularly relevant and deserve some additional comment.

## Bulls, Bears and Pigs

There is a stock market adage that says "the bears get some, the bulls get some, and the pigs get none." Like most adages, there is a great deal of truth in this one. Just to refresh your memory: the bull is the investor who feels there is inherent value in a particular stock or a particular segment of the market, and buys on that basis; the bear is the opposite, he feels a particular stock or segment is overpriced and he wants out — but he's still an astute, informed investor. The pig, on the other hand, is the gambler who wants as quick and as huge a profit as he can possibly make and who buys and sells irrationally with the predictable result that over the long run pigs lose money.

However, the existence of the gambler in the market (and there are some observers who insist there are more gamblers than true investors or speculators) has an enormous impact on excessive rises and declines in common share prices.

The difference between the gambler and the investor is that the gambler does not have the patience to wait for inherent value to be reflected in stock prices. If the stock doesn't go up quickly, the gambler unloads, regardless of the underlying values of the stock.

## Emotion

Even real investors sometimes let their emotions overrule their logic.

There aren't many veteran investors who have not, at some time in their careers, made one or both of the following common emotional errors: when earnings are on the up-swing, assume that the rise will continue and pay too much for the stock; or, in a year when earnings fall, panic and sell at a low point, then watch the stock recover nicely over the next few months.

Either of the foregoing scenarios has an exaggerated effect on market prices. The main point is not to panic because of a market swing, if it is a swing caused largely by investor psychology. On the bright side, wide swings in prices offer opportunities to make money. Be a bull, then a bear — but, never a pig.

## World Events

It is difficult to understand why some world happenings affect common share prices, but they surely do. Strikes, U.S. presidential elections, war threats, peace offerings, OPEC decisions, assassinations, and countless other events and non-events all send the stock market into a frenzy.

Investors must remember that, as Bernard Baruch put it half a century or so ago, the stock market is the thermometer, not the fever. There are so many factors affecting common share prices that the real investor must always consider the long-term and not be stampeded by favourable or unfavourable news with only short-term implications.

## Long-term Factors

Economic trends, quality of management, technological advances, new discoveries, strike vulnerability, new products, raw material supplies, transportation, distribution, and population shifts are all important factors affecting the inherent value of a stock which will have long-term effects. Factors such as these should be given far more weight by the investor than investor psychology or world events having short-term implications. For the speculator, of course, the reverse is true.

Decisions to buy or sell common shares should be made on the basis of sound business judgment. In addition to the factors listed in the preceding paragraph, consideration should also be given to: current yield and price/earnings ratio; the financial condition of the corporation; the capitalization of the corporation; and the marketability of the shares.

# FACTORS TO CONSIDER BEFORE INVESTING

The Canadian Securities Institute wisely and correctly suggests five main factors to be reviewed when deciding whether to invest in the common shares of a particular company.
They are:

1. the nature and characteristics of the industry,
2. the past performance of the industry,

**3.** the future of the industry,

**4.** the position of the company in the industry, and

**5.** the relative performance of the company compared to other companies in the industry.

## Nature of Industry

It's important to understand the nature and characteristics of the industry in which you're investing in order to match your investment objectives with the probable behaviour of common share prices. For example, retired people (whose investment objectives are income and protection of capital) would not want to invest heavily in an industry which is subject to wide, cyclical fluctuations in stock prices, such as the construction and building supplies industry.

On the other hand, a young investor looking for substantial growth in a portfolio would likely stay away from an industry characterized by higher income and slower growth, such as public utilities.

There are a number of main industry classifications in which a person can invest through the ownership of publicly-traded common shares in this country. For example:

**1.** the automobile and allied industries,

**2.** banking and finance,

**3.** chemicals and allied industries,

**4.** computer services,

**5.** construction and building supplies,

**6.** electronics,

**7.** entertainment and leisure,

**8.** food and beverages,

**9.** forest products,

**10.** heavy machinery and equipment,

**11.** insurance,

**12.** iron and steel,

**13.** mining,

**14.** oil and gas,

**15.** printing, publishing and broadcasting,

**16.** public utilities,

**17.** real estate,

**18.** textiles, and

**19.** transportation.

An additional category is the public investment or holding company through which indirect investments can be made in some or all of the above industries.

Knowing the characteristics of an industry aids in evaluating problems or opportunities likely to be encountered by a particular company and which might have a significant effect on share prices. For example, the general level of interest rates greatly affects the construction and building supplies industry. The state of technological advance can make or break a company in the field of electronics.

There is a wealth of information available about industry sectors. The larger brokerage houses will always be pleased to provide you with data on particular industries. Most industry sectors have their own organizations — such as the *Canadian Manufacturer's Association, Mining Association of Canada, Canadian Textile Institute, Canadian Bankers' Association,* and the *Housing and Urban Development Association of Canada,* just to name a few — which will also be pleased to help you to learn about their particular industries. In addition, most public companies will be delighted to help you learn, not just about their own company, but their particular industry as well, by sending you reading material.

### Past Performance

Although most relevant when considering well-established companies with a long record of earnings, the past performance of an industry can often offer important clues to the future potential of a particular industry or company.

The key is to spot trends, either favourable or unfavourable, and then try to establish the underlying reasons behind the trends. This information can then be used to determine the direction the industry is apt to follow. These conclusions are then used as a backdrop against which knowledge of particular companies within the industry is considered. If you spot a trend early enough, you are in a position to make money by buying shares during a favourable trend and to maximize your gain by getting out early when things are beginning to look bad.

### Industry Outlook

As important as past performance is, it would be unwise in the extreme to make an investment without giving great consideration to the future. Some factors which might have a drastic effect on a particular industry are:

1. government intervention and legislation,
2. technological advances,
3. new products,
4. population shifts, and
5. competition.

### The Company Itself

Having satisfied yourself that the outlook for a particular industry is bright, attention should then be turned to the factors which pertain to the particular company whose shares you are considering buying or selling.

In addition to its financial position, capitalization and management, the company's place in the industry and its relative performance vis-à-vis competitors must be evaluated. In doing this always remember it is often necessary to study more than one industry. Many companies today are so diversified that they span many industry classifications.

When comparing the relative performances of two or more companies — after considering their financial position, capitalization and management — there are other major areas to consider, such as: sales, profit trends; tax rates; return on equity; cash flow; dividend record; price-earnings ratio; and, marketability.

## OBJECTIVES

Overriding everything, though, is your own investment objective. Be sure what you buy is consistent with your goal. There are three major possible objectives:

**1.** security of capital,

**2.** income, and

**3.** growth.

Of course, in many instances an investor will try to achieve more than one objective. This can usually be accomplished. Right now you might want to re-read Chapter 16, where investment objectives are discussed in detail.

## Speculating

Now a word for the speculator. Some people may assume that share speculation is bad. Not so. The rookie speculator should, though, follow these rules:

**1.** recognize the difference between speculating and investing, and don't confuse one with the other;

**2.** speculate only with money you can afford to lose;

**3.** deal only with reputable investment houses;

**4.** judge each issue on its own merits; and

**5.** always ignore tips and rumours.

# chapter twenty

# *Preferred Shares*

## WHY PREFERRED SHARES?

Like other forms of investment vehicles, the preferred share
evolved to meet the needs of the issuer on the one hand and the
desires of investors on the other. For example, the preferred share
is attractive for investors interested in a security providing less
uncertainty than common shares but who also prefer an equity
(share) position to holding debt.

From the issuer's standpoint there are any number of reasons
why the preferred share route might be chosen rather than a debt
issue or the issue of additional common shares. An obvious disadvantage of issuing additional common shares is the dilution of
existing shareholdings. In other cases market conditions might be
unfavourable for the issue of new stock.

Once the decision has been made not to go the common share
route, the reasons for a preferred share issue rather than a debt
issue come into play and are more varied. For example, the corporation's assets may already be fully pledged so that it has no room
for an additional mortgage bond issue, or the corporation may be
in a type of business that has few pledgeable assets, such as a
finance company. On the other hand, the market may simply be
temporarily unreceptive to new debt issues or perhaps the issuing

corporation hasn't yet established a sufficiently high credit rating to sell unsecured debentures.

Sometimes the issuing corporation's board of directors makes an outright unilateral decision to issue preferred shares rather than additional debt or common shares regardless of what the outside market forces might seem to dictate. The board might simply want to balance the corporation's capital structure, or they might want to avoid fixed interest obligations on new debt. Furthermore, issuing preferred shares rather than debt often avoids a fixed maturity date. A board of directors will sometimes postpone payment of a preferred dividend, but will go to any length to avoid missing an interest payment or maturity date. Indeed, the effect on the public of missing or postponing a deferred dividend is nothing compared to the trauma of a missed interest or redemption date.

The immediately foregoing comment notwithstanding, investors shouldn't automatically assume a sinister motive when preferred shares are issued rather than common shares or debt. On the other hand, the prudent investor will restrict his investment in preferred shares to those of high quality issues who have earnings available for dividend payments well in excess of the minimum requirements insisted on by informed investment analysts. Later on we discuss ways of evaluating the quality of a particular preferred share issue. For now, back to a description of the actual position of preferred shareholders.

The preferred shareholder is a hybrid occupying a position between a common shareholder and a creditor. If the corporation falls upon evil times the preferred shareholder is in a better position than a common shareholder but is not as well protected as a debt holder.

As their name implies, preferred shares carry with them certain preferences which are not available to the common shareholders. These preferences can, and will, vary from corporation to corporation and even from one issue to another of the same corporation. (A corporation can, and often does, issue more than one class of preferred shares.) The point to keep in mind is to determine exactly what the preferences are and how they should affect your investment decision.

The most common preference given on preferred shares is a prior claim on the assets of a corporation ahead of the common shareholders in the event the corporation is wound up. In these circumstances creditors rank first, preferred shareholders next, and the common shareholders get what's left — if anything. By *quid pro quo*, the preferred shareholder gives up any claim on corporation earnings beyond the stated dividend, whereas once creditors and preferred dividends are satisfied the common shareholders can theoretically pay the balance of earnings to themselves as dividends.

Preferred shares normally have a par value and the preference as to asset distribution is usually that amount in the event of an involuntary liquidation, and par plus a small premium where the liquidation is voluntary. It's probably fair to say, though, that situations where this particular preference is of importance are apt to be situations which you should avoid.

Preferred shares usually carry a fixed dividend rate expressed as a percentage of the par value. Like all dividends, these too have to be declared by the board of directors and can only be paid from current or past earnings. However, another common preference is that no dividends can be paid to common shareholders if preferred dividends are not.

Many preferred share issues carry a provision entitling preferred shareholders to elect one or more directors to the board to represent their interests if dividends are in arrears or have been omitted. In some cases the preferred shares become fully voting when dividends have not been paid. These provisions usually apply only after a stipulated number of consecutive dividends have been missed — for example, two or three.

Let's now take a close look at the variety of types of preferred share issues which exist. Although the number of preferred share features is limited only by the bounds of the issuers' imaginations, there is a very definite limit to the number of variations which investors will buy. Accordingly, the vast majority of preferred share issues carry with them one or more of a few fairly well established characteristics.

## Votes

Preferred shares are generally non-voting. But, they can be voting and they often carry with them provisions which cause them to become voting in certain circumstances — the most common of which is, as just mentioned, when dividends are in arrears. It is a rare situation, though, when control of a public company is affected by votes of preferred shareholders.

However, preferred shareholders are usually granted a vote on matters affecting the underlying quality of their security. Examples would be an increase in the amount of preferred stock authorized or the creation or increase of funded debt.

## Cumulative and Non-Cumulative

A cumulative preferred share is one for which a record is kept of any dividends that have not been paid and on which the accrued amount of such dividends must be paid before payment of any dividends to the common shareholders or before any preferred shares can be redeemed by the issuing corporation.

Of course, a non-cumulative preferred share is one for which the shareholder is entitled only to dividends which are actually specifically declared. If a dividend on a non-cumulative preferred share is passed, it's gone forever and does not accrue.

Although in theory some cumulative preferred shares with dividend arrears might be worthwhile speculative investments, there isn't exactly a bull market for those issues.

## Participating and Non-participating

Participating preferred shares carry with them rights to partici-pate in the issuing corporation's earnings over and above their stated dividend rate. For example, an issue of participating pre-ferred shares might share equally with the common shares in any dividends paid over, say, two dollars per share on the common.

Sometimes the participation is limited. For example, the par-ticipating preferred share might be entitled to a specified cumula-tive dividend of $1.00 per year, after which each common share is entitled to a dividend of $1.00 in a particular year, then both classes share dividends equally until an additional $1.00 is paid on each in that particular year, after which the preferred shares would no longer be entitled to further dividends in that year.

Again, the obvious: a non-participating preferred share would be limited to the specified dividend regardless of the level of divi-dends paid to the common shareholder.

## Callable or Redeemable

Callable  or redeemable preferred shares are redeemable at the option of the issuing corporation during a specified period of time for a specified price. The callable price is never less than par and it is quite common for the issuer to pay a small premium upon calling in the shares as compensation to the investor for giving up the investment. Also, any unpaid accrued dividends would be included in the amounts received by the preferred shareholders upon giving up their shares in these circumstances.

## Retractable

In a manner of speaking, retractable preferreds are the opposite of callable or redeemable shares. The holder of retractable preferred shares has the right to tender his or her shares to the issuer for redemption, again at a specified price and time. So, you, the investor will know when you will give up your shares. On the other hand, redeemable securities are redeemed at the option of the issuer. You really have no choice in the matter.

## Convertible

A conversion feature gives the shareholder the right of converting preferred shares into another security — usually common shares — of the issuer. Again, this must usually happen during a specified time period and on specified terms.

## QUALITY OF PREFERRED SHARES

There are four key questions to be considered when attempting to judge the investment quality of a particular preferred share issue.

The first question is: do the issuing corporation's earnings provide ample coverage for the payment of preferred dividends and meeting any relevant redemption or retraction provisions?

The next question is: has the issuing corporation established a good record of dividend payments?

Third: is there an adequate cushion of common share capital beneath the preferred shares?

Finally: was the security sponsored and underwritten by a reputable investment dealer?

Remembering that investments are made in preferred shares by investors whose goal is income and security rather than potential capital gains, you see that "yes" — or, at least, "probably" — has to be the answer to all of these questions before the particular issue would qualify as a high-quality investment. Let's now examine some of the rules-of-thumb used by many financial analysts in answering those questions.

For these and other such tests mentioned in this book, always remember that there are no foolproof methods of testing the quality of an investment. The tests suggested are some of the types most commonly used by investment analysts. But, to repeat, when it comes to evaluating investments, nothing is foolproof.

Now that you have the warning that excess use of these tests may be dangerous to your wealth, we should quickly add that they are extremely useful if not relied on in the extreme.

Oh, yes. To do these tests you will need a copy of the company's most recent annual report. Annual reports are easily obtained by writing or calling the company itself. *The Financial Times of Canada* and *The Financial Post* both have services through which they supply copies of many public companies' annual reports. And, finally, your broker will almost always be able to supply them to you. As a matter of fact, your broker should be pleased to perform these tests for you. If not, consider finding a broker who will.

## Adequacy of Dividend Coverage

The first test suggested was a determination of whether the issuing corporation's earnings provide adequate coverage for preferred dividend requirements. Because preferred shareholders are in a weaker position than creditors, the minimum requirements for a preferred investment must be higher than those for bonds or debentures.

There are two usual methods of calculating dividend coverage of preferred shares: the simple method and the prior charges method. The simple method is used where the corporation has no funded debt outstanding. As the name implies, it is a fairly simple formula consisting of net *earnings before extraordinary items* divided by *annual preferred dividend requirements*.

In corporations where there is a large proportion of debt relative to preferred share capital outstanding, the simple method can be very misleading. For example, the simple method might, in these circumstances, show the preferred dividend coverage to be many times greater than the interest coverage on long-term debt.

This could lead to the ridiculous conclusion that the preferred share is of a higher investment quality than the bond.

This would hardly be the case because during a financial squeeze the corporation would always pass on declaring a dividend rather than miss an interest payment. In such circumstances, the prior charges method — although slightly complicated — is a truer picture of the margin of safety.

## Prior Charges Method

This procedure requires the application of a formula which is a bit complicated. However, as mentioned earlier, your broker will be delighted to do this calculation for you, and this is one that might best be left up to him or her. But, for those of you who want to give it a go, here's how.

The formula for the prior charges method can be expressed as *total income after operating expenses* divided by *interest and preferred dividends before tax*. It is the denominator of that formula, when the formula is expressed as a fraction, that provides the complication. Because preferred dividends are paid after income taxes, the calculation is made on a before-tax basis. This requires the preferred dividend figure to be adjusted by the appropriate rate of income tax that the corporation usually pays.

To be precise about this, two mathematical steps are required. You first solve the following equation:

$$\frac{\text{income tax}}{\text{net earnings before extraordinary items} + \text{income taxes}} = \text{tax rate}$$

Then:

$$\text{actual preferred dividends} \times \frac{100}{100 - \text{tax rate}}$$
$$= \frac{\text{preferred dividends}}{\text{before tax}}$$

It is the *preferred dividends before tax* figure so obtained that is added to *interest* in the denominator referred to earlier. If you find this too complicated, ask your broker to do it for you.

This brings us naturally to the question of what is adequate coverage once you've calculated it.

### Adequate Dividend Coverage

Of course, adequate dividend coverage can't be defined precisely, if for no other reason than the fact it varies from industry to industry and even from corporation to corporation.

For large corporations which are prominent in their respective industries, the Canadian Securities Institute suggests the following minimum coverage: Public Utilities — 2½ times under the simple method and 1½ times under the prior charges method; Industrials — 4 times under the simple method and 2 times under the prior charges method. Preferred investments in cyclical industries — e.g. textiles — should be watched carefully if the coverage is near the minimum.

Remember, too, that this is only one of our main suggested tests and the foregoing minimums are a rule-of-thumb only, but, a good one.

### Dividend Payment Record

The second main test is whether the corporation has established a good record of dividend payments. The easiest and most reliable source of this information is the annual report or your broker. No special knowledge or formulas are required to assess this information. The corporation's record is either good, bad, or something in between.

### Equity Backing

The third test is equity backing. In a good quality situation the equity per preferred share would not be less than the par value of the shares, and ideally there should be a solid cushion behind each share issue over at least a five-year period. For a top quality rating the equity per preferred share should be on a rising trend.

### Dealer Sponsorship

Underwriting by a reputable investment dealer indicates that a thorough investigation of the merits of the proposed preferred issue was carried out and that experts in the field (the dealers) are satisfied the issue is at least worthy of inclusion in some investors' portfolios.

It's up to you and your advisors to determine whether it should be in yours.

In reaching your preferred share investment decisions, you should not rely solely on the four key questions dealt with above. There are definitely other factors which must be taken into consideration. Indeed, in any individual's circumstances one or more of the following factors may turn out to be more critical than the four so-called key tests.

### Eligibility for Insurance Investments

Some investors place a lot of emphasis on whether the issue is an eligible investment for life insurance companies without recourse to the basket clause. If it is, this is usually an indication it is a reasonably solid investment.

The basket clause is a provision in the *Canadian and British Insurance Companies Act* which allows a life insurance company to invest up to a particular percentage of the book value of its total assets in investments not otherwise qualifying under the principal conditions of the Act. At the time of writing, to qualify outside the basket clause, full preferred dividends would have to have been paid for each of the five years immediately preceding the date of the insurance company making the investment.

### Protection

The protections built into the preferred share issue should be examined and evaluated. For example, sometimes consent of two-thirds of the preferred shares outstanding is required before the issuing corporation would be allowed to sell or transfer substantial property. A similar consent might be required before the issuer could consolidate or merge with another company whose securities would rank prior to or with the existing stock.

It's not unusual for a protective clause to restrict the creation of other preferred shares senior or equal to the existing issues to situations in which prior approval of the current preferred shareholders has been obtained or certain specified financial conditions have been met.

Amendments to provisions of a class of preferred shares normally require the consent of a stated percentage of the outstanding preferred shares.

A very common protective provision is one designed to ensure that the issuer's working capital is not seriously depleted by the payment of dividends on common shares.

Ask your broker to explain in plain English what the protective provisions of a particular issue are.

## Marketability

Marketability may be the most important consideration for many investors. Key considerations are whether the shares are listed on a stock exchange and whether they are widely traded. Even if they are traded publicly — either listed or over the counter — that is of small consolation if they are so thinly traded that there is effectively no buyer when you want or have to sell.

## Funding

The very existence, and terms thereof, of any sinking fund (funds systematically set aside to redeem shares or pay off debt) or purchase fund could be an important consideration for some investors. However, if most other considerations suggest a good quality issue, not too many potential investors would back off simply because there is no sinking fund.

## Market Price vs Call Price

Another area of possible concern is the relationship between the market price of an issue and its call price. You should hesitate if the market price is higher than the call or redemption price, unless there's a good explanation as to why, such as an unusually high dividend with a long time to go before redemption can be triggered. Naturally, conversion terms or retractable features must be examined in relation to the market price.

## The Issuer

Most important of all, of course, is a general evaluation of the issuing corporation itself, its financial health, its trend of earnings, and to the extent feasible, its market position and its management capabilities. This is a tall order and the vast majority of investors must rely on expert analysis by experienced investment counsellors and dealers. But, the information is available and the careful investor makes every reasonable effort to obtain as much information as possible.

Making investments without attempting to gain as much relevant information as possible is really speculation. As already mentioned, speculation has its place, but it's critical that you are not speculating when you think you are, or should be, investing. There's a vast difference.

## The Main Point

Preferred shares are designed to meet particular needs of issuers and are of interest to certain types of investors. Be sure you have a good fit. They are not suitable if you are looking for capital growth situations, but are usually attractive for the person who wants a relatively safe equity position providing a reasonable level of income.

You should always examine and understand the characteristics of the particular issue being considered. It's rare for any two issues to be identical.

You should evaluate the issuing corporation to the best of your ability or obtain the opinion of experienced, professional investment dealers or counsellors — preferably both.

You should also pay particular attention to the protective features of the issue in addition to the so-called key tests for evaluating an issue. You must satisfy yourself regarding the factors, such as marketability, which may be of particular importance to you.

Because there is no contractual promise to pay off the preferred shares, and most corporations would miss a dividend before missing an interest payment, preferred shares carry more risk than bonds and debentures. The best bet is to restrict preferred investments to those whose dividends are well covered by earnings and assets.

On the positive side, their preferences as to dividends and claims on assets make them safer investments than many common shares — but, remember the growth potential isn't as great as with common shares.

Higher quality preferred shares are a good income investment with a significant degree of safety. But always remember, there is always some risk involved no matter how small. It is always possible for a company to fail so utterly that even the preferred shareholders get nothing or little back.

# chapter twenty-one
# *Bonds and Debentures*

## WHAT ARE THEY?

A bond simply represents a loan made to the corporation or government body that issued it.

There are differences between bonds and debentures on the one hand, and shares or stocks of a company on the other. A stock represents an actual interest in the ownership of a corporation whereas a bond, as already mentioned, is evidence of a debt. A debenture is a type of bond, usually used in reference to municipal or unsecured bonds.

The issuer promises to repay the face amount of the bond (which is not necessarily what you paid for it) on its maturity date, and in the meantime, to pay interest on it. In terms of investment objectives, high quality bonds and debentures usually provide greater protection of capital and certainty of income than common or preferred shares. On the other hand, there is usually less prospect for capital growth with bonds than with common shares and in times of rising interest rates the marketability of bonds is poor. However, bonds purchased at deep discounts or carrying with them warrants or conversion features, often provide an opportunity for capital appreciation.

Issuers of bonds sometimes reserve the right to pay them off before maturity, which they would do should interest rates drop. This is usually accomplished by the issue of a callable or redeemable bond. The issuer normally agrees to give a reasonable notice — say, 30 or 60 days — to the bondholder that the bond is going to be redeemed. If you are making an investment in particular bonds and you want to ensure it remains a long-term investment, then be sure the bonds are not subject to an early redemption.

The amount which the issuer of a bond agrees to pay on maturity is shown on the face of the bond itself and is referred to as its denomination, par, or face value. The smallest corporate bond denomination is usually $500. Denominations of $1,000, $5,000, $10,000, $25,000 and even $100,000 are common. The intended market will indicate the denomination. Bonds designed for a broad retail market will be issued in small denominations (for example, Canada Savings Bonds have been issued in denominations of $100 to accommodate the small investor) while those designed for institutional investors might be made available in denominations reaching into millions of dollars.

In addition to the denomination, the face of the bond will also state the rate of interest payable. Remember, though, that the interest rate is applied to the face amount of the bond, not to the amount you pay for the bond.

The price paid for a bond will depend not only on its denomination but also on its stated interest rate, the general level of interest rates at the time it is purchased, and the length of time to maturity. Prices of outstanding bonds tend to fall as general interest rates rise and go up when interest rates go down. For example, if you are holding a $1,000 bond with an interest rate of 6% at a time when the interest rate for term deposits is 12%, no one would pay you $1,000 for that bond. They would only pay the amount that would give them a return of 12%. This brings us to bond yields — the figures that really count.

Bond yield is the true rate of return received on the amount of money invested, which is the price paid — not the bond's denomination. For example, if a $100 bond with a 7% interest rate is purchased for $99 and that bond matures in a year, your yield will be 8%. The 8% consists of $7 interest and $1 "gain" on principal. Now, assume you had to pay $101 for the same bond. Your yield now drops to 6% — $7 interest less a $1 "loss" of principal. Obviously there would be a wider variation in yield if the term is lengthened and the bond is purchased at a higher discount or premium. A 7%, $100 bond due in ten years and purchased for $94 would yield an annual rate of about 7.9%. Fortunately, although bond yield calculations are complicated, you need not worry about doing them because any investment dealer will have bond yield tables readily available.

Of course, yield is not the only consideration in making your decision whether to invest in a particular bond. The investment quality of the bond or debenture should also be considered. Indeed, this aspect will also have some bearing on the yield available for the simple reason that the higher the quality the lesser the discount or greater the premium.

## VARIOUS TYPES

There are four major classes of bond issuers: the federal government, the provinces, municipalities and, of course, corporations. We'll now turn to the qualitative considerations of each type.

So far as the quality of Government of Canada bonds is concerned, if the federal government ever defaults on its bonds, it's hard to imagine the total chaos that would be existent throughout the entire Canadian investment community. Most investments would be in jeopardy.

There are three main considerations in judging the quality of a particular provincial bond issue. You should consider how much the province already owes, and how much it will owe after the particular issue, on a per capita basis in comparison to other provinces. The next consideration is just how well off the province is in terms of natural resources, agricultural production and industrial development. And, finally, consider the stability and soundness of the provincial government, historically and potentially as well as currently. The best guide to the value of this type of security is the advice of an experienced investment dealer who specializes in the field. On balance, provincial bonds are considered to be pretty reliable investments in terms of safety of capital.

With some bad experiences having been reported in the United States, many people became a bit reluctant to invest in municipal debentures. To date in Canada, investment dealers and institutional investors (pension funds, insurance companies, etc.) tend to consider municipal debentures in much the same category as Government of Canada and provincial bonds. They look upon them as very high grade investments as regards safety of capital.

Investment dealers and institutions do have a checklist for rating the quality of municipal bonds. They consider such items as population growth, industrial growth, condition and quality of municipal services, ratio of annual debt charges to total revenue, tax levies, tax collection record, assessed value for tax purposes per capita, debt per capita, and the integrity and experience of elected municipal politicians and senior civil servants. As in the case of provincial bonds, the best way to get an accurate reading on the quality of municipal debentures is through the advice of an experienced specialist in that field.

## Corporate Bonds and Debentures

Each year Canadian corporations issue billions of dollars worth of bonds and debentures, normally to acquire fixed assets, retire existing debt or expand their businesses.

With the passage of time, different types of corporate debt securities (always remember that a bond or debenture is nothing more or less than evidence of debt which is owed by the issuer to the holder) are designed to help bring the needs of the corporate borrower in line with the desires of the investor-lender. In colloquial terms it's a case of different strokes for different folks. In any event, investors who are interested in the bond market should be familiar with the different types of debt securities and their various characteristics. Following is an analysis of the most common types.

## Mortgage Bonds

Any mortgage is a legal document evidencing that the borrower (the mortgagor) has pledged fixed assets such as land, buildings and equipment, as security for a loan and entitling the lender (the mortgagee) to take ownership of the properties pledged if the borrower fails to pay the interest or repay the principal when due. There is no basic difference between the legal effect of a mortgage and mortgage bond. The only difference is in the actual form of the document.

The mortgage bond, like other forms of corporate debt securities, evolved to fill a particular need. When the borrowing requirements of corporations became too large to be financed by one source, and many hundreds — indeed many thousands — of lenders became involved, it became impractical for a corporation to issue separate mortgages securing portions of its properties to each lender, and the mortgage bond was born. What happens is one blanket mortgage is deposited with a trustee, usually a trust company, and that trustee acts on behalf of all the investor-lenders in protecting their interests under the terms of the blanket mortgage. The total amount of the loan is divided into appropriate denominations and each investor receives a bond as evidence of his or her pro rata claim under the terms of the blanket mortgage.

This brings us to the various sub-types of mortgage bonds.

### First Mortgage Bonds

As the name implies, first mortgage bonds are the senior securities of a corporation for the simple reason that they constitute a first charge on the corporation's assets and earnings. Of course, it would be necessary to study the terms of the issue to determine specifically which properties are covered by the mortgage. Anyone who has tried this will quickly recognize the difficulty of understanding the legalese in which the terms are drafted. They rival the *Income Tax Act* for sheer incomprehensibility. This is another instance where your best bet is to rely on the advice of a specialist in the field.

When the legalese is stripped away, you usually find that most first mortgage bonds carry a first and specific charge against the corporation's fixed assets and a floating charge (a general claim on assets without attachment to specific items) on all other assets. First mortgage bonds are generally regarded as the best security a corporation can issue. This is particularly true if the mortgage contains an "after-acquired clause." This is a stipulation that the mortgage applies to "all fixed assets of the corporation now and hereafter acquired." It's desirability from the investor's standpoint is obvious from the wording of the phrase itself.

In short, first mortgage bonds have a prior claim over other classes of debt security, which, depending on the quality of the corporation itself, makes them a high quality investment.

For the record, it should be mentioned, though, that in some circumstances a corporation may, with the consent of existing first mortgage bondholders, issue what are referred to as prior lien bonds. The effect of such a move is that the first mortgage bond-holders allow the prior lien bondholders to share a specific claim on the corporation's assets.

## Second or General Mortgage Bonds

As you would logically expect, second mortgage bonds — often referred to as general mortgage bonds — rank after first mortgage bonds in any claim on assets or earnings of the borrowing corpora-tion, meaning that the claims of the first mortgage bondholders must be settled in full before there is anything left for the second or general bondholders. Because the situation results in the second mortgage bonds being somewhat of a lower quality from an investment protection standpoint, they usually sell at a price that gives a higher yield than first mortgage bonds.

Actually, in many circumstances the asset coverage on first mortgage bonds is so good that the quality of a second or general bond issue is equal to the senior bonds. For example, sometimes a corporation with an existing first mortgage issue will float an issue of general mortgage bonds secured by its own unpledged assets and those of its subsidiaries. Although the new issue would be junior to the first mortgage bonds as far as the parent company's assets are concerned, the new issue would have a prior claim on the assets of the subsidiaries. In fact, it was just this type of issue which gave birth to the term "general mortgage bond."

As the titles of mortgage bond issues can be at best confusing and at worst misleading, it is advisable to check the terms of the issue if the priority of claim to assets is of particular interest or concern to you. It is better still to obtain the advice of a knowl-edgeable expert.

## Debentures

As mentioned earlier, debentures represent direct debt obligations of the issuer, but they are not secured by the pledge of assets. In fact, their only security is the general credit of their issuer. Holders of debentures have no prior claim on assets as against other gen-eral creditors. Should you come across the term "secured deben-tures," it is not a complete contradiction in terms. This term is applied to debentures which are partly secured by particular assets, but not sufficiently covered to constitute a full mortgage.

The absence of an underlying pledge of assets doesn't necessarily mean the debenture is of a lesser quality than a bond. What you must look at is the reason a debenture rather than a bond is being issued. It could be one of a number of perfectly acceptable reasons and it is important to ascertain which one applies in the particular circumstances.

For example, a well established, large, successful corporation may have such a good credit rating that it is able to borrow money on favourable terms without having to pledge any of its assets at all. A corporation might be large, successful and perfectly solvent but not have sufficient assets to pledge due to the nature of its business, which is frequently the case with commercial or mercantile operations, whose only significant assets are those in which they trade and therefore cannot easily be pledged. To cite an extreme example, Eaton's could not be expected to pledge their inventory — they have to be able to sell it. Nor would it be reasonable to expect the Bank of Montreal to pledge its deposits. You would not likely assign a lower quality rating to debentures vis-à-vis bonds in either of these circumstances.

On the other hand, a corporation with a heavy investment in fixed assets might be going the debenture route because all its assets are already pledged as a result of earlier bond issues and mortgages. In these circumstances, unless there were compensating factors such as a top credit rating and excellent long-term prospects for the company, you should consider the debenture to be a cut below a bond and either pass up the opportunity or seek a higher return to offset the higher risk.

"Subordinated debentures" are, as the name clearly implies, debentures which are junior to some other security of the issuer. Once again, the possibility exists that this type of issue is not top quality and the advantages of obtaining expert investment advice before putting up money for a subordinated debenture are obvious.

## Income Bonds or Debentures

Generally speaking, income bonds or debentures are bonds or debentures in the ordinary sense except that interest is not payable on them unless the issuer has earned profits sufficient to cover the interest thereon. In this connection "profit" is usually defined by the terms of the issue and may not be the generally accepted definition of the word, so be sure to check it out carefully.

Furthermore the term "income bond or debenture" has a specific meaning under the *Income Tax Act* and special income tax treatment may apply. Accordingly, this is one type of investment that is clearly suitable only for the very sophisticated investor and should never be undertaken without the benefit of expert investment and income tax advice.

## Sinking Fund Bonds

These are not securities issued by steamship companies or oil well diggers — not necessarily, that is.

A sinking fund is a sum of money or pool of investments earmarked to provide resources for the redemption or retirement of a bond issue. A sinking fund reserve is the portion of earnings earmarked for the purpose of establishing and expanding the sinking fund. It is a means of providing for the ultimate payment of the debt on a piecemeal basis each year throughout the term of the particular debt rather than by re-financing it all when it comes due.

Usually a trust company is appointed as a trustee to administer the fund. On a fixed date each year the borrower provides the required amount (which might include bonds of the particular issue concerned, which the issuer reacquired) to the trustee who will invest and hold it in trust for the ultimate redemption of the issue. The borrowing corporation will no longer have any control over the funds.

Bond issues which carry sinking fund provisions usually indicate this fact in their title. The significance to you as an investor is assurance that money is being set aside which can be used only to redeem your securities.

## Collateral Trust Bonds

A collateral trust bond is secured, not by a pledge of fixed assets, but by a physical pledge of other securities. For example, a corporation issuing a collateral trust bond might pledge as security bonds or shares of other corporations. It's a situation similar to an individual pledging securities to a bank to secure a personal loan.

You might think the quality of this type of bond is lower than a mortgage bond — but that's a dangerous generalization. Sometimes the pledged securities are of such a high quality themselves that the collateral trust bond is just as secure.

Occasionally, to provide an even greater than normal security for a mortgage bond, collateral in the form of other securities is also pledged. This type of issue is usually referred to as a "mortgage and collateral trust bond."

### Extendible Bonds and Debentures

These issues usually have a relatively short maturity term, say, five years, but carry with them the option for the investor to exchange them for a longer term debt, say, 20 years, at the same or a slightly higher rate of interest.

You will usually have to make your decision during an election period usually beginning from one year to six months before the original maturity date and usually lasting about six months. If you take no action your bonds will automatically mature on schedule. The advantage to the investor is that you will have more time to make your decision as to how long you wish to commit your funds, but will still have your money working for you in the meantime.

### Retractable Bonds and Debentures

As you may have already guessed, these issues are the exact opposite of extendible bonds or debentures. These are issued for a long term, say, 20 years, but you have the option of turning in the bond for redemption earlier, say, after 10 years. As in the case of extendible bonds, the election period usually lasts for six months and begins from one year to six months before the earlier, retraction period expires. Once again, if you do not elect, the bond matures on the original maturity date — in this case, 10 years later.

The quality of a bond is not affected by these special features — although the rate of interest would be — and you are still going to have to look at the underlying security and credit rating of the issuer to completely satisfy yourself. Extendible and retractable issues are appropriate vehicles for the investor who wants an investment which is not purely short-term, but also wants to retain flexibility in avoiding a very long term.

Extendible and retractable bonds and debentures are sometimes issued by governments as well as by corporations.

## Serial Bonds and Debentures

With these types of issues some of the principal comes due and is
paid off each year on a predetermined basis. Individual investors
don't usually buy into the short maturities of a serial issue. They
are usually of interest (no pun intended) to institutional investors
looking for short-term situations. As the burden of debt decreases
and the interest cost is correspondingly reduced each year, the
quality of the remaining longer-term outstanding bonds tends to
improve.

## Convertible Bonds and Debentures

Convertible bonds or debentures carry with them a right allowing
them to be exchanged for common shares of the issuer under specified terms. A convertible issue combines some of the advantages of
both debt and share ownership. Because they have a fixed interest
rate and a definite maturity date, they possess the advantages of
bonds and debentures. On the other hand, they offer possibilities
of obtaining capital appreciation through the option to convert
them into common shares at a predetermined price over a stated
period of time.

From the issuer's standpoint the conversion feature makes an
issue more saleable at a lower borrowing cost while at the same
time raising equity capital indirectly on more favourable terms
than through the direct sale of common shares.

Although the heading above refers to both bonds and debentures, issues of convertible bonds are really quite rare. The investor looking to combine safety and certainty of income of a corporate debt instrument with the prospects of future capital growth
will likely have to settle for a convertible debenture. This is
because it is easier to arrange a convertible issue which is not
secured by specific assets.

Often, the conversion price increases with the passing of time.
This encourages earlier conversion and reflects the fact that most
companies' net worth grows with the passage of time. Always
remember, though, that it makes no sense whatever to invest in a
convertible debenture if the conversion price is higher than the
present and probable future price of the underlying share.

Convertible issues require a little more babysitting than most investments because their prices are more volatile and decisions whether or not to convert must be made. You also don't want to miss any time deadlines.

In addition to the investment quality of the debenture itself, the price level of the underlying common shares also affects the price of the debenture. Normally, when the underlying stock is well below the conversion price, the convertible debenture behaves like any other bond or debenture by responding to the general level of interest rates and the quality of the security. When the underlying stock is near to the conversion price the debenture usually sells at a premium, and when it rises above the conversion price the debenture should rise correspondingly in price.

To take a simple example, assume a $100 debenture allowing you to convert to ten common shares. Assume further that the interest rate on the debenture is comparable to that obtainable from alternate sources. When the common shares are trading around $10 each there will probably be a premium of a dollar or two attached to the debenture so that you could sell it for, say $102. If the common shares were trading at $12 each, the debenture is obviously worth close to $120 — the value of the common shares into which it can be converted. On the other hand, if the common shares are trading at $6, the conversion feature has no value.

## Debentures with Warrants

A warrant is a certificate giving the holder the right to purchase stock (normally one common share) at a specified price over a stated period of time. Warrants are sometimes attached to debentures to make them (the debentures) more saleable and, of course, may themselves be bought and sold on stock exchanges or over-the-counter.

Warrants are a very attractive investment vehicle. If the warrant allows you to purchase the relevant common shares at a price below the going market price, you have two favourable options available to you. You can either purchase the shares at a bargain, or if you don't want to hold common shares in that particular company, sell the warrants themselves at a profit.

Buying and selling warrants will often allow you to make as much profit at much less risk than in dealing in common shares. For example, if a stock costing $25 goes up to $30 you would have

to risk $5,000 to make $1,000 (200 shares x $25). If there were war-
rants available allowing the purchase of that stock at $25, they
would rise in price by about $5 each as well. So, if you bought
those warrants at, say, $10 and sold them at $15, you could make
$1,000 by risking only $2,000 (200 shares x $10).

# INVESTMENT QUALITY OF BONDS AND DEBENTURES

Judging the investment quality of a corporate bond or debenture is
difficult. Many investment analysts use five main rules-of-thumb
(in the form of questions to be answered) to assist in making such
an evaluation. As you review these now you'll see they are quite
similar to the rules-of-thumb for evaluating preferred share issues.

### Interest Coverage

Do the corporation's earnings provide sufficient coverage for the
payment of interest and repayment of principal?

The Canadian Securities Institute offers the following
formula to use as a test:

$$\frac{\text{total income after operating expenses}}{\text{total interest requirements in latest fiscal year}}$$

And, although quick to point out that adequate coverage can't be
defined precisely, the C.S.I. does suggest the following minimum
standards for interest coverage:

Public Utilities: current year's interest should be covered at
least two times by the average annual earnings available in the
last seven-year period.

Industrials: current year's interest should be covered at least
three times by the average annual earnings available in the last
seven-year period.

When it comes to repayment of principal, you must consider
the level of interest coverage and the ability to meet sinking fund
requirements — especially what emergency measures might be
available to the corporation, such as eliminating a dividend on
common shares. However, another consideration in this connection is the next rule-of-thumb.

## Asset Coverage

Do the assets pledged offer sufficient security? is the next question, and suggests you might get a plausible answer by dividing total long-term debt by net tangible assets. (Generally speaking, net tangible assets are total assets less intangible assets, current liabilities, deferred income taxes, other credits and minority interests.)

Minimum standards suggested by the C.S.I. are:

Public Utilities: $1,500 of net tangible assets per $1,000 of outstanding debt.

Industrials: $2,000 of net tangible assets per $1,000 of outstanding debt.

However, remember that most balance sheets do not reflect the increase in price levels since assets were purchased. They're usually shown at cost.

## Debit/Equity Ratio

Probably the best known of the five tests, the debt/equity ratio answers the question: is there a large enough cushion of equity capital beneath the bond or debenture issue?

The C.S.I. suggests, as a minimum, that a corporation's long-term debt should not exceed the current market value of all the corporation's outstanding classes of stock. This is a very good rule-of-thumb, particularly in circumstances where the results of the asset coverage test may not be satisfactory.

Another advantage of this test is that it reflects a decline in the earnings of a corporation because this fact itself would cause a decline in the market value of the corporation's stock.

## Dealer Sponsorship Test

In many cases this is the only test which individual investors ever apply — simply answering the question: was the security sponsored and underwritten by an established, reputable investment dealer? A "no" answer here is cause for pause, while a "yes" answer is a good indication that the security has been thoroughly investigated and found to be soundly constructed. It is reasonable to expect the issuer will be able to meet its obligations in respect to both principal and interest.

## Eligibility for Life Companies

The last question is: is the security eligible for investment by a life insurance company without recourse to the "basket" clause? This requires some explanation.

The types of securities in which life insurance companies may invest are classified by the *Canadian and British Insurance Companies Act*. Eligibility under this Act is a favourable factor in determining investment quality as long as eligibility is not achieved under the Act's basket clause. The basket clause allows up to a particular percentage of the book value of a life insurer's total assets to be invested in investments which would not otherwise qualify under the principal conditions of the Act.

## Other Factors

In addition to the five foregoing tests (note that a "yes" answer is desirable for each question; a "no" is bad news) there are other factors which should be taken into consideration when evaluating the quality of a particular debt security. These include: the trend of earnings over the past seven to ten years; interest coverage (see page 178) in the year of lowest earnings; the nature of the corporation's industry in light of the economic outlook; and, sinking fund and other protective provisions.

## Protective Provisions

This is the term applied to the features of a particular security designed to protect the interests of the investors. For example; prohibition of prior liens; restrictions on additional borrowing; sinking fund provisions; and, requirements that dividends not result in the reduction of the corporation's working capital below a stated amount.

## Caveat

The C.S.I. is careful to caution users of their rules-of-thumb that mechanical standards are far from foolproof when it comes to rating securities. There exist qualifying factors which are not measurable by statistical means, the most important of which is the quality of the corporation's management. Another example is the progress, or the lack thereof, of the natural business cycle and the effects of general economic swings.

## Objective

Never lose sight of the real objective of investors who buy bonds and debentures. They are looking for safety of capital and certainty of income. The best way to achieve this objective is to ensure there is an adequate margin of safety in the particular security.

## Canada Savings Bonds

Canada Savings Bonds, in effect, give you an interest income on cash in your wallet. This is so because they can be turned into cash at any time simply by presenting them to your bank.

As for security, nothing is better. If the Government of Canada defaults, it is hard to conceive of any investment being any good.

In determining whether the rate of return is adequate, you should compare it to what is available on daily-interest savings accounts, not term deposits or other investments which are less liquid than Canada Savings Bonds.

Canada Savings Bonds are an excellent investment to make while you're learning more about investments generally.

# chapter twenty-two

# *Annuities*

## VARIOUS KINDS

Webster defines an annuity as "an amount payable yearly or at other regular intervals." If only it were so simple! When you go to buy an annuity, you are suddenly confronted with an array of products that truly boggles the mind. Too often people make a bad choice rather than suffer the embarrassment of admitting they don't understand all the terms and buzz-words which characterize various annuity options.

This chapter examines some of the more common options available and what they normally mean. Even this approach is fraught with danger because there are over 100 insurance and trust companies offering annuities for sale in the country, and they don't all call the options the same thing. But, as cowardice is seldom rewarded, here goes.

### Immediate Annuity

With any annuity the income payments received may be monthly, quarterly, semi-annual or annual. They have to be at least annual. Theoretically, the payments could be received weekly or daily, but any payment period less than monthly is rare, if indeed any exist at all.

If the annuity is an immediate annuity, the payments begin immediately — well, almost immediately. The point is they aren't deferred for any significant period of time. For example, if an immediate annuity is purchased on July 23rd, payments would likely begin no later than September 1st, and possibly even as early as August 1st.

The amount of the income you will receive is determined by the amount paid for the annuity.

### Deferred Annuity

Just the opposite of the immediate annuity, payments out of a deferred annuity will not begin until some specified date in the future. They might begin on a date determined by a particular number of years, such as 5, 10 or 15 years after purchase. Or they might begin on a date determined by the purchaser's age, such as at age 50, 60 or 65.

Once the annuity starts to pay, the payments again can be monthly, quarterly, semi-annual or annual, and their amount will be determined by the premium paid for the annuity plus a stipulated rate of return thereon throughout the deferral period.

### Life-Only

Under this type of annuity the purchaser receives payments only as long as he or she lives. Because the annuity holder's beneficiaries will receive nothing from the annuity after the annuitant dies, the return on this type of annuity is usually higher than on any other.

But, it's shooting dice. The purchaser is really betting against the insurance company and the stakes are high. If you live longer than the mortality tables suggest, a gain will be made at the expense of the issuer. On the other hand, if you die the day after buying the annuity it's a total loss.

It's a rare set of circumstances in which a life-only annuity is appropriate, but the fact there still exists a market for them is testimony that some investors go that route. Probably the same ones who visit Las Vegas regularly.

## Life with Guaranteed Period

If you're looking for income for life but want to hedge your bets against the total downside risk inherent in the life-only annuity, the life annuity with a guaranteed period is the way to go.

Under this type of annuity, payments will be made as long as you live, but should you expire before the guaranteed period does (which can be many years, depending on a number of circumstances), the annuity payments will continue to be made to your beneficiary for the unexpired portions of the term.

## Annuity Certain

With an annuity certain, payments will be made for a specific number of years — normally, 5, 10 or 15 — regardless of how long the purchaser lives. Suppose you buy an annuity certain for a 10-year period. At the end of the 10 years the payments stop. If you die before the 10 years are up, payments will continue to be made to your beneficiary throughout the balance of the 10-year period.

## Joint and Survivor Annuity

Under a joint and survivor annuity, payments will be made for the balance of your life and will continue to be made to your beneficiary for the rest of his or her life. Of course, if your designated beneficiary dies before you, the annuity payments will end upon your death.

## Impaired Life Annuity

Often overlooked in financial planning, the impaired life annuity should be considered in appropriate circumstances. If for some reason a person's life expectancy is significantly shorter than normal, upon receipt of adequate medical evidence an insurance company may provide considerably larger life annuity payments than in ordinary circumstances, because the issuer can reasonably expect to pay them for a much shorter time period. This is the reverse effect of being "rated" for insurance purposes.

## Life Annuity Specially Guaranteed

Still another hybrid. The option offered by a life annuity with a special guarantee is as follows. Should you have the misfortune to die before receiving annuity payments equal to the purchase price of the annuity, the difference will be paid to your beneficiary either as a lump sum or in periodic installments.

### Variable Annuity

The variable annuity option is really one which can be tied to any of the above. The annuity ultimately chosen can, if you wish, be tied into a variable factor — such as prime rates of interest or a stock or mortgage fund — which will increase or decrease the annuity payments according to the performance of the fund or rate to which it is tied. In the absence of choosing such an option, you would know exactly how much your annuity payments would be.

### Difficult Choice

Considering that the foregoing is not a complete list of available options, and that many of them can be combined to create still more choices, it is obvious that the selection of an annuity must be made with great care and always in the light of your own particular circumstances. There is no general rule. However, if you want to consider extremes, just to put the matter in perspective, a middle-aged, perfectly healthy individual would most likely be better off in the long run with an annuity for life; whereas a Hollywood stuntman would be well advised to always insist on a guaranteed term of fifteen years.

Shop carefully, consider all alternatives and be absolutely certain that you understand all the terms, and their implications, of the type of annuity you finally settle on.

# chapter twenty-three
# *Options*

This chapter does not deal with stock options in the sense of those which are offered to employees by corporations, but rather the options which can be traded on the major stock exchanges by buying and selling options issued by Trans Canada Options Inc. on the shares of certain corporations.

Dealing in options is a way to "invest" in high priced shares without having to put up amounts of money equal to the value of the underlying shares. However, it is also a way to get completely wiped out very quickly.

Basically, options work this way. Brace yourself to learn a few technical terms here; options have their own jargon. A call option is a contract allowing you to purchase a given number of shares in a company within a set period of time at a given price. The shares in question are called the underlying security; the price at which you are allowed to buy them is the exercise price or premium. Option contracts are usually for 100 shares, so multiply all prices by 100. Once issued, options trade on the market just as stocks and bonds do, until they expire.

Equipped with that basic information, you can now read the options listings in your daily newspaper.

Suppose you see this listing:

| Option | Volume | Last | Close |
|--------|--------|------|-------|
| X Ltd. | | | |
| Jul 27½ | 10 | 3¼ | 28⅜ |

The option is to buy 100 common shares of X Ltd. at a price of $27.50 each before the end of July. Ten option contracts (each for 100 shares) were traded on the previous day and the last option traded sold at a price of $3.25 per share, or a total of $325 for one option contract. The "close" column refers to the previous day's closing price of the underlying security — $28⅜.

Obviously, investors are expecting X Ltd. stock to rise; they are willing to pay $3.25 for the chance to buy a share at $27.50, which brings the total price they would pay (if they exercised their options) to $30.75 plus commissions. They could buy X Ltd. shares more cheaply than that on the open market at $28⅜. So why buy options? The simple answer is that if X Ltd. shares go even higher — say, to $33 — they will make money because their total purchase price is still only $30.75

On the other hand, if the shares fall to, say, $25, no one in his right mind will want to exercise the option. But even if an investor misses a chance to sell the option and has to let it expire, the total loss is still only $325 — the price paid for the original contract instead of $2,837.50 – $2,500 = 337.50 (or much more if value went down even further). In other words, for a relatively small capital input you get a chance to make a large profit (but not as large as if actual shares had been bought at $28⅜).

Don't think you now know enough to rush off and place a large options order with your broker. If you do, the first thing he or she will do is give you a copy of the prospectus of the Trans Canada Options Inc., then tell you to go away for at least two days and read the prospectus, plus some other material you will be given. It will really take you weeks to read it.

Your reading will open up a whole new — and confusing — world. First you will be introduced to the concept of the clearing corporation. In one sense, the clearing corporation is simply the options exchange. But it also plays a far greater role. In order to understand this, you will have to digest some more jargon. Essentially, the clearing corporation is the middleman between holders and writers of options.

Holders are the people we discussed above — the buyers of

option contracts. But they have to buy their options from some-body; that is where the writer comes in. A writer is an individual who undertakes to sell a given number of shares at a set price within a set period (the duration of an options contract is usually three, six or nine months). In return for this promise — that is, in return for writing the option — the writer is paid a premium. (Essentially, the premium is determined by the market.)

This is where the clearing corporation comes in. It acts as the middleman between writer and buyer. And, what is much more important, once the option has been issued, the clearing corpora-tion assumes final responsibility for the contract.

It works this way. Suppose you have 100 shares of X Ltd. which you bought at $47 and which are now sitting at $45. You would like a little extra money but don't want to take a capital loss by selling the shares. So you tell your broker that you are willing to write an option to sell your shares at $50 any time within the next six months, and that for this you would like a premium of $2.50 a share. Your broker notifies the clearing corporation, which then finds a buyer who is willing to buy the option at that price. You immediately receive $250 ($2.50 each for 100 shares) but you still have your shares.

If the holder (or other holders who buy the option on the market) does not exercise the option, you have nothing to worry about. You have your shares plus $250. If, on the other hand, it is exercised, you have $250 plus a capital gain of $3 a share. But sup-pose that X Ltd.'s stock has suddenly become the hottest thing in the market and you think it's going to go away up. You've changed your mind and you don't want to sell your shares at $50. What to do?

Simple. You buy another option to pick up 100 shares of X Ltd. at $50, thus offsetting your earlier commitment to sell your own shares; your broker notifies the clearing corporation that you have thereby made a closing purchase transaction. Now, when the holder of the option you originally wrote arrives to exercise it, the clearing corporation (and not you) is responsible for seeing that he or she gets shares. You are in the clear.

In this particular example, you have been a *covered writer* — a writer who actually owns the shares you are contracting to sell. If you are a conservative investor you probably will be happiest being a covered writer. If you have a more daring streak, you may wish to be an uncovered writer — that is, to write the option without actually owning the shares. The risk here is, of course, that if the option is exercised you will be caught having to buy the shares on the open market for more than the option holder is going to pay for them, which makes the whole deal a lot more speculative. It's all perfectly legal, just risky. You would only do this if you are willing (and able) to gamble that the price of the underlying stock is going to fall.

If you want to be a holder rather than either kind of writer, that generally is still more speculative. The risk, of course, is that your option will expire before the underlying stock price gets where you expected it to. Remember that an option is a wasting asset — it will vanish completely at the end of its term. And remember also that as the expiry date nears, the market price of options generally declines. If your timing is bad you can lose your shirt.

Options investment strategies are numerous. If you are interested, your broker can provide information about rising and falling market strategies, variable protection, "straddles" and a host of other approaches. But those probably should be attempted only by fairly sophisticated investors. For most, a few basic strategies are sufficient. And it is essential to bear some key points in mind:

1. The options market is very risky. You can minimize the risk, but you cannot eliminate it.
2. Timing is everything. It is not enough to guess right about the price trend of a stock; you must also guess right about when that trend will develop.
3. The Canadian options market, though growing, is still small. This means that buyers or sellers may not always be there when you want to unload or buy an option. And you almost certainly will want to sell it, if you are a holder. Only a small percentage of options are actually exercised. They are not, by themselves, investments. If you were really interested in the stock you probably would buy it in the first instance. Most holders make their money by trading, just as in the stock market.

Incidentally, "put" options are the opposite of "call" options. With a "put" option the writer undertakes to buy stock instead of selling it.

Many astute financial advisors suggest the following guidelines for dealing with options:

1. Never *buy* an option.
2. Restrict your selling to covered writing (as described above).

On the other hand, if you want to speculate you can make a lot more money with less invested by trading options rather than the actual stock.

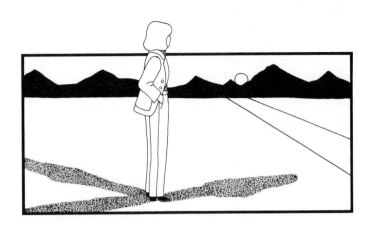

# chapter twenty-four
# *Diversification*

## WHY DIVERSIFY?

The second most difficult problem investors face — second only to actually picking the right investments —is deciding what proportion of their total funds should be committed to particular types of securities, or any other investment for that matter. Spreading investments among various types of securities is normally referred to as diversification. The difficulties of diversification are matched only by the importance thereof, because diversification of holdings is the only way to reconcile the incompatible objectives of safety of capital, income and growth.

An investment policy is not sound unless diversification is an integral part. This is because any investment in publicly-traded securities always carries with it an element of risk, and it is clearly good strategy to spread that risk over a number of different securities. If investments are distributed over a number of securities and one of them performs badly, only some of the investor's capital is affected. Furthermore, in a diversified holding, the odds are that some securities will do better than expected. This will offset losses incurred by those in the portfolio which do not perform as well as expected — and the odds are there will be some of those, too.

There are really two headings under which diversification should be discussed: risk reduction and investment convenience.

## Risk Reduction

For most investors, reduction in risk is the compelling reason for diversifying their holdings. There are essentially four ways to reduce risk through diversification.

The first is to limit the amount of money you put into any one investment. When confronted with an investment opportunity that looks particularly attractive, the temptation to plunge in completely is often overwhelming — but, it is a temptation that must be resisted. Regardless of how good a particular issue looks, it is normally wise to spread your capital among a number of issues of different quality or rank. In this way diversification strengthens your overall position without making any great sacrifice of income, marketability or possible capital growth. If your main objective is income, your capital risk is greatly reduced through diversification.

The second way is to distribute funds among particular issues of similar quality in a number of corporations of similar rank engaged in the same kind of activity. For example, the bonds of a number of public utilities, governments, etc., could be purchased in preference to putting all your cash into the bonds of one utility. If diversified, you don't depend on the fortunes of one entity.

The third method of reducing risk through diversification is to invest in corporations that are engaged in different types of businesses. The advantage of this type of diversification comes from the external conditions which often influence an entire industry. For example, while a general recession affects most industries to some extent, there is no doubt it affects some more severely than others. Public utilities and food and beverage industries tend to continue to hold their own, relatively speaking, during a recession. On the other hand, a recession usually has a more drastic effect on the lumber, construction, real estate and heavy manufacturing industries. And, there is everything in between. The advantages of diversification are fairly obvious in these circumstances.

Consider, too, that holdings in a number of industries operating in various parts of the country — or in various parts of the world, for that matter — will provide even greater protection through ownership in a cross-section of businesses augmented by geographical diversification.

Another form of diversification falling into this category is to devote a portion of your funds to providing straight income, while using the rest to seek capital appreciation by investing in growth stocks.

Although risk reduction may be the prime objective, the principle of diversification will allow you to invest in securities which themselves carry an element of risk without sacrificing the safety of your entire bundle, while at the same time possibly increasing your total investment income.

The fifth method of reducing risk through diversification, and one favoured by a great number of investors, is investing in holding or investment companies.

The classic holding company scenario features a corporation with a very high capitalization that purchases shares of a number of operating companies in various industries that may or may not be related. The holding company is non-operating in the normal sense, but the really big ones usually participate, indirectly and in varying degrees, in the management of companies in which they invest through the provision of managerial talent and technology.

Another method of diversifying this way is to buy shares in a mutual fund. Mutual funds will be discussed in greater detail a little further on. For now, back to holding companies.

The diversification advantage is obvious. In addition, by investing in one or more holding companies, a small investor is able to invest in several industries that might not otherwise be available due to sheer cost. As a case in point, a single investment in Canadian Pacific would automatically put you into the railway, oil and gas, mining, hotel, real estate, logging, food, and iron and steel industries. This, too, is an obvious advantage of diversification.

Purchasing shares in an investment fund is the easiest and often the most practical method of diversifying investments. Generally speaking, an investment fund is a company whose business is the investing of its capital, raised through the marketing of its own shares, in various securities. It is structured much like any other company, but instead of using its capital to build a plant, purchase raw materials and hire employees, it invests it in stocks and bonds of other companies with an eye to earning income in the form of dividends and interest, and making capital gains through timely switches in the securities owned. After administration expenses are paid from these earnings, dividends are distributed to the investment fund's shareholders or re-invested.

It is obvious, then, how the investment fund differs from an operating company. What is not so obvious, though, it how it differs from a holding company. The distinction is that holding companies, such as Canadian Pacific, although their business is investing in other companies, usually become substantially involved in the management of the companies whose shares they hold. Investment funds do not, primarily because they want to be able to quickly and completely dispose of their holdings on short notice, a move which would be inconsistent with the holding company concept.

Another distinction between the holding company and the investment fund is that the holding company's investments are not nearly as diversified nor do they cover as wide a range as those of an investment fund. And, of course, the investment fund's portfolio changes almost daily, whereas the holding company normally holds its investments for many, many years — in some cases, it seems, forever.

## MAIN CATEGORIES OF INVESTMENT FUNDS

There are two main categories of investment funds: closed-end funds and open-end funds: the latter are more commonly referred to as mutual funds.

Both types of funds raise capital by selling their own shares and debt securities to the public. However, the closed-end fund raises a particular amount of capital and operates at that level, plus retained earnings, for an extended period of time, much like an operating company. If you want to buy or sell shares of a closed-end fund, you normally have to make the transaction with other buyers or sellers through a stock exchange or on the over-the-counter market.

Mutual funds, on the other hand, continually issue their own treasury shares to as many investors and in whatever numbers the market will bear. Similarly, the mutual fund will redeem its own shares on demand. Therefore, the mutual fund's shares are bought from and sold to the company itself rather than from and to other shareholders.

Although the market price of the shares of a closed-end fund is obviously affected by the market value of the securities held by the fund in its own portfolio, the closed-end fund shares themselves usually trade at a level somewhat below their net asset value, because buyers and sellers must be found in the open market. This, too, is in direct contrast to the behaviour of mutual fund share prices. The price of a mutual fund stock has a direct relationship to the net asset value of the fund's portfolio because the fund will redeem its own shares on demand at a price based on its current net asset value.

Because investment in mutual funds are more common than in closed-end funds, the following comments on diversifying through the use of investment funds will be restricted to mutual funds.

## Mutual Funds

There are four major types of mutual funds:

**1.** balanced funds;
**2.** income funds;
**3.** equity funds; and
**4.** specialty funds.

Balanced funds, as the name suggests, represent the ultimate in investment diversification. Their portfolios are spread among common shares, preferred shares, bonds, debentures, and other commercial paper. A typical split — depending on current financial market conditions — might be: common stocks 60%; preferred shares 20%; bonds 7%; commercial paper 10%; and, cash 3%.

Income funds concentrate more on bonds and debentures, with some high-grade preferreds but very few common shares. Their goal is high income and safety of capital.

The equity fund is the most popular type of mutual fund and it invests primarily in common shares with the goal being growth of capital.

Then there are the specialty funds. These funds concentrate on a specific industry, for example: oil and gas; gold; chemicals; steel; or, perhaps a particular geographical area, such as U.S. or European investments. There are also specialty funds that concentrate on mortgages and others that deal exclusively in money markets.

To make the description complete, two other types of funds, though extremely rare and forming a small part of the present total fund picture, should be mentioned.

The first of these is the speculative fund, euphemistically referred to in some quarters as a "performance fund." These funds invest in high-risk, speculative common stocks. The poker table, race track and Las Vegas may be better bets.

The other type of fund, once popular but now also relegated to the weirdo class, is the fixed fund. In this fund, top-quality investments are chosen and just left there with little or no turn-over. The advantage is minimization of management and adminis-tration costs. The obvious disadvantage, and no doubt the cause of their almost total extinction, is that things simply change too rapidly in this day and age to make that approach a sensible form of diversification.

## INVESTOR CONVENIENCE

If you're relying on investment income for your living expenses, you're going to want to receive dividend and interest payments spread throughout the year rather than all at once.

This is usually accomplished in one of two ways: according to maturity dates or the distribution of income receipts throughout the year.

The value of a debt security at the time of its maturity is usu-ally its par or face value. If debt securities' values always remained stable at their par or face value, maturity dates would be irrele-vant. But that's not the way it is. Changing business and economic conditions cause interest rates to fluctuate, and the government often forces interest rate changes upon an unwilling market. When interest rates rise, bond prices fall and vice versa.

The closer a bond is to its maturity date, the closer its price will be to its par value, and it follows that its price fluctuation will be within a very narrow range. Also, short-term bond prices usually don't fluctuate as widely as do long-term bonds.

Because you can't tell with certainty what business and eco-nomic conditions will be at any particular time in the future, it makes good investment sense to vary maturity dates so that the bulk of your portfolio doesn't fall due at the same time.

Furthermore, the date of maturity is usually the date you will re-invest your money. Recognizing that the market may be especially good at one time and particularly bad at another, the ideal situation would be to have only a small portion of your portfolio coming due at any one time.

Although a minor consideration for many investors, for others the spreading of dividend and interest income as evenly as possible throughout the year is of significant importance. This is the case for investors who use their investment income for personal and living expenses, much like salary. For them a steady stream of income is essential.

Because interest payments on bonds are usually made semi-annually and dividend payments on both common and preferred shares range anywhere from quarterly to annually, it is possible, by exercising some care in security selection, to distribute income receipts fairly well throughout the year.

## OVERDIVERSIFICATION

Like all good things, diversification can be overdone. It should be kept within reasonable limits and what is reasonable in diversification, as is the case with so many investment decisions, depends entirely on an individual's particular circumstances. But, there are some general comments which can be usefully made.

An important point to remember is to deal as much as possible in board lots when buying or selling stocks. An investor will usually have to pay a higher price (with a possible higher commission cost) for odd lots (less than a board lot). And it is a no-win situation. Paradoxically, an investor will usually receive less for an odd lot when selling. This happens because it's unlikely that there will be an odd-lot buyer available at exactly the same time as there is an odd-lot seller, so the price must go up or down depending on which party is compelled to sell or buy as the case might be.

Another key point is that the number of stocks you can know well and follow intelligently is limited unless you make managing your investments a full-time job. Not many people have the time and resources to achieve such a lofty goal.

A good rule-of-thumb is to limit investment in any one security to 10% of your total portfolio.

Then there is the administration aspect. A lot of capital spread over a large number of small investments requires a lot of careful supervision and is often inefficient in the long run.

For the average investor — say, up to $50,000 — ten different securities is an adequate and quite manageable diversification program. It's hard to imagine an investment of less than $1,000 in one security making any sense. Of course, this particular rule-of-thumb does not apply to speculative purchases.

Although the really big investor who manages his or her own affairs could realistically be investing in 20 or more different securities, the 10% rule is a good one for investors of all sizes.

The main point to remember is to avoid a portfolio that looks like a mini stock exchange. In these circumstances the investments will seldom do better in the long run than the market average — and that's not usually good enough.

## Balance

As mentioned previously, it is impossible to maximize all of safety of capital, receipt of income, and capital growth within any one portfolio. What is possible, though, is to balance a portfolio to maximize one particular objective without completely sacrificing the other two.

The make-up of a portfolio can, and should, change from time to time as individual requirements and economic conditions change.

There are numerous examples in circulation of so-called illustrative portfolios. They serve a useful purpose as a starting point — but only as a starting point — in determining what yours should look like. It is absolutely essential to fine tune the portfolio to your own requirements and economic circumstances.

# chapter twenty-five

# Commodities, Collectibles and Precious Metals

## COMMODITY TRADING

The commodity market — whether we are speaking of precious metals, or the more common commodities such as coffee, potatoes and grain products, or for that matter the esoterics, like pork bellies — is no place for the amateur or the faint of heart.

People must realize, before getting into it, that commodity trading is the most speculative of market activity and is in no way an investment activity. The commodities market is dominated by experts in the various fields, and is a game in which the casual player can be wiped out very quickly.

In this book, in the parts dealing with investments in securities, it is pointed out that one of the important factors affecting the stock market is investor psychology. In the commodity field, *speculator* psychology is a major force — about on a par with earnings per share in the stock market. Add to this the fact that many commodity prices are affected by, of all things, the weather in various parts of the world, and you have some feeling for what you're up against. Can you really handle the strain of knowing that the safety of your money depends on what the weather is going to be like next fall in Brazil?

Does this mean no one should ever put money into the commodities market? Of course not. What it does mean, though, is that no one should get into commodities trading until he or she has acquired an in-depth knowledge of the particular commodities chosen and how the markets for those particular commodities work. You see, the commodities market is not just one market. It's many markets. Each commodity has its own market and its own market influences.

For example, let's get back to the weather in Brazil. If you decide you're going to trade in the coffee market, that's a commodity and that's a separate market. You don't really buy and sell coffee. What you buy and sell are contracts to purchase or sell coffee at some later date. You might, for instance, buy a contract which allows the holder to buy or sell a certain amount of coffee a number of months from now. The price you will pay for that contract is based on the best guess by you and other players as to what coffee will be worth at that time. Your hope is that the price will move in whatever direction is needed to make your contract (either to buy or sell) worth more. Two things to remember here. First, the other players in the coffee market fall into two categories: speculators, like you or me, who are really guessing; and, coffee dealers, the people who really buy and sell coffee as well as deal in pieces of paper like we would be doing, who probably have a lot better handle on what the price is apt to do than you or I. Second, the whole deal may rise or fall on the coffee crop in Brazil. That, in turn, could depend strictly on the weather down there. Or, the attitude of the Brazilian government.

It is no different if you're dealing in potatoes or wheat. Even professional climatologists have difficulty predicting the weather in Prince Edward Island and Saskatchewan. Not to mention Idaho, Maine and Russia.

One thing you should understand about the commodities market, though, is that you aren't dealing in the actual commodity itself. You are dealing with contracts to buy or sell it sometime in the future. That's why it's often referred to as the "futures" market. It works somewhat like the stock options market described on pages 186-90. It's hard to imagine what would have to go wrong before you'd end up with a truck dumping a couple of tons of pork bellies on your front lawn.

What is not difficult to imagine is the complexity of the

markets and the tremendous odds the amateur player is bucking at all times.

The only thing certain about commodities trading it that you should do so only with money you can clearly afford to lose. It's an area best left to experts. And you don't have just my word to take for it. One chairman of the Commodity Futures Trading Commission in the United States upon leaving office was quoted by *The Wall Street Journal*. He said, "I have never, ever, been in the futures market myself; I don't have the skill for it."

## COLLECTIBLES

Much has been written and spoken in recent years about investing in collectibles — things like works of art, stamp and coin collections, Persian rugs and china figurines.

The first thing to remember about this activity is that it is *not* investing. It may be a business, it may be speculation, it may be spending money for the sheer enjoyment of the items themselves, but it is not investing.

There is absolutely nothing wrong with buying any of these things with a view to making a profit on them someday as long as you realize that this is speculation. And, of course, there is nothing wrong with buying such items for their sheer enjoyment, and if you make money on them later on, all the better.

The reasons they do not qualify as investments in the context of this book follow. First, they do not provide any regular income. Bonds pay interest and many stocks pay dividends. Real estate can be used to provide rental income. But, works of art and collections of any kind do not produce regular income. In fact, they cost money in the form of insurance, cost of storage, and income foregone on the cost. Second, they are very illiquid; very hard to sell at a profit when you want to. When it comes to collectibles, it is almost always impossible to get the price you want when you want it, unless you are a dealer. Another problem in the area of collectibles is the very high commissions you must pay, whether you are buying or selling.

Still another problem with collectibles is the simple fact they are extremely sensitive to trends. The hot print or limited edition book of today may be tomorrow's garage sale item.

Now, none of this negative commentary means that you

should never buy a piece of art or that you should avoid collecting things you enjoy. By all means do so if you have the money to spend and the personal interest necessary to understand and enjoy whatever it is you are collecting. But, do not consider this to be a part of your investment activity. At best, it's speculation.

## PRECIOUS METALS

Like the collectibles dealt with in the preceding section, there has been a great deal said and written about making money by investing in precious metals, such as gold or silver, and similar commodities such as diamonds. Indeed, fortunes have been made by some people in these endeavours. But, many more fortunes have been lost.

Again, like collectibles, and like commodity trading, this is really an area of speculation rather than investment, except, of course, for the professional trader — but, then that's a business, not an investment.

Getting involved in the precious metal market is definitely not for the unsophisticated. Nor is it a sensible move for anyone who is playing with money that he or she can't afford to lose. In order to make money as a trader in precious metals you have to have a fair amount of money that you can clearly spare because you cannot afford to have to sell at a time other than of your own choosing. The swings in the market for these commodities are so wide and unpredictable that you simply have to be able to wait out the bad times or you will lose your shirt.

The people who were buying gold at $60 an ounce were ecstatic when the price hit $400. But, the poor wretches that bought it at $900 an ounce didn't share the same feeling when *they* had to sell at $400.

The odds are that you will be far better off to leave this one to the professionals as well.

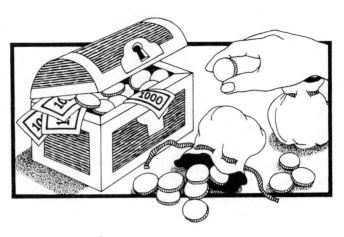

# chapter twenty-six
# *Treasury Bills*

Back in March 1980, the Bank of Canada began basing its bank rate (which, of course, ultimately dictates the interest rates for all Canadian financial institutions) on the average rate established in the weekly tender for 91-day treasury bills issued by the federal government. Instead of the Bank of Canada making announcements from time to time as to what the rate would be, since March 13, 1980, the rate is set at one-quarter of one percentage point above the treasury bill average rate. The new bank rate is announced at 2 p.m., Eastern Time, each Thursday.

In 1980 Canadians suddenly became aware that there were these mysterious things called treasury bills and that every Thursday they were auctioned off, probably in some well-guarded vault with walls six feet thick and money all over the floor, amid the racket of auctioneer's gavels and frantically shouted bids from hordes of hysterical financiers. Even now, many Canadians still think that's the way it is.

Well, it's a shame to blow away the mystique, but the fact is Government of Canada treasury bills are nothing more or less than simple negotiable bearer promissory notes issued by the federal government to obtain working capital. And, the auction is held at the Bank of Canada building in Ottawa. Not only is there no money on the floor, there are no gavels, no auctioneers and the bidders aren't even there.

Here's what really happens. First, a bit about the treasury bills themselves. They are, as already mentioned, promissory notes issued in denominations of $1,000, $5,000, $25,000, $100,000 and $1,000,000. There are two types of treasury bills issued weekly, one with a term of 91 days and the other with a term of 182 days. Treasury bills with a term of one year are issued every four weeks.

The bills themselves do not carry a specific rate of interest. Rather, they are sold at a discount with the yield to the purchaser determined by the difference between the price paid and the par value which will be received upon maturity.

To take a very simple example, assume a bidder acquires a $1,000, 91-day treasury bill for $970. He pays $970 for the bill on, say, July 17th. On October 15th he will have the bill redeemed and receive $1,000. So, he has made $30 in 91 days on an investment of $970. That's an annual return of 12.4%.

If the 12.4% represented the average rate established in the weekly tender of treasury bills on July 17th, that afternoon the Bank of Canada would set its bank rate at about 12¾%.

The amounts and the maturity dates of the bills to be offered are announced a week in advance and the Bank of Canada, acting as an agent for the federal government, calls for tenders.

The chartered banks, about a dozen or so of the largest investment dealers in the country, and the Bank of Canada itself, regularly submit tenders at the weekly auction. However, any bank or investment dealer on the list of "primary distributors" (a list, it is understood, containing about 100 names) is eligible to bid.

The potential buyers submit their bids, normally by sealed tender, to the Bank of Canada in Ottawa. This cannot be done until noon, Eastern Time, on the day of the auction. Representatives of the Department of Finance and the Bank of Canada receive the bids. Some bidders tender a single amount and others tender bids covering a range of prices.

The highest bidder receives all of the bills it bid for at that price, then the second highest, and so on until the entire issue has been sold. Although a potential buyer can submit more than one bid, the top bid is considered first. It is possible that a bidder could have all bids accepted and acquire several bills with the same maturity, each at a different price. If the amount of bids at the lowest successful price exceeds the total of the issue remaining, that remainder is allotted on a pro rata basis among the participants who submitted bids at that price.

Settlement, both payment and delivery, must be completed by 3 p.m. the following day.

The Minister of Finance always reserves the right to accept or reject any tender in whole or in part. Furthermore, in addition to bidding for bills it wants to buy, the Bank of Canada may, if it wants, tender a reserve bid for the entire issue. Although on the one hand this allows the government to effectively continue control of the central bank's interest rate, it does guarantee a market for the entire issue and prevents any group from forcing a significant reduction in the price of the bills either by boycotting the issue or forming a syndicate to submit low bids.

It must never be overlooked though, that this procedure provides the federal government with an effective mechanism by which to exert an enormous effect on all interest rates. This is particularly so when the Bank of Canada's rate is tied to the weekly auction, but even in the absence of that, the weekly treasury bill auction has been, is, and will likely continue to be, the single most important influence on all short-term interest rates.

Okay. So, we now know treasury bills are usually acquired by the chartered banks and large investment dealers. But, then what happens to them?

Well, in the case of the chartered banks, as a rule they are simply kept until they are redeemed upon maturity. This is so because they constitute a very important part of the chartered banks' legally required reserves.

Investment dealers, on the other hand, buy the bills primarily to sell on the secondary market to investors having excess cash to invest for a short term. Such investors include commercial and financial institutions, municipal and provincial governments, foreign investors, other dealers, corporations and the Bank of Canada itself. As a matter of fact, unsuccessful bidders at the weekly auction usually enter this secondary market immediately in order to meet their particular requirements. This second phase of the weekly auction is usually more lively and interesting than the original auction.

Apart from the chartered banks, large corporations are probably the most active investors in treasury bills. They acquire their bills in the secondary market from the investment dealers and find them to be particularly attractive short-term investments. Not only can they be acquired in amounts suiting any particular treasurer's needs, but maturity dates (ranging from a day or two up to a year) dovetailing nicely with any date on which a particular corporation needs its cash back are normally available. Furthermore, treasury bills are as close to a riskless investment as can be found. And, they are totally liquid.

That is another reason why they are so important to the Canadian money market. They provide a ready and relatively easy means for the free movement of money from places in which it is not needed for the time being, to places where it can be put to work effectively.

But it is only the really big individual investor who is able to invest directly in treasury bills. As mentioned earlier, individuals are not involved in the weekly auction. Therefore they have to make their treasury bill investments by dealing with a broker in the secondary market described above. Normally brokers prefer to deal in units of $250,000. They will, on occasion, drop down to $100,000, but at that level the yield to the investor is not necessarily better than he or she can achieve in other types of investments. So, it can be seen that the only direct significance of treasury bills to the vast majority of Canadians is the fact that it is the treasury bill rate which sets the level for most other interest rates in the country. But, that fact alone is sufficiently important to warrant an understanding of how treasury bills work.

The yields on new treasury bills, of course, vary from week to week and are extremely sensitive to all changing credit conditions. However, an investor's yield is set at the time of purchase because, although it is bought at a discount, maturity at full face value is assured. Accordingly, the sensitivity does not result in uncertainty.

There is no doubt as to the importance of treasury bills in the total Canadian money market, and although they have become household words only in the 1980s (because of the Bank of Canada's interest rate being tied to them), they've been around for a long time.

Canadian treasury bills, payable in sterling, were sold on the London market and in continental Europe in the early 1900s. Beginning in 1914, they were sold to Canadian chartered banks, but there was no secondary market. Then in the mid-1920s the issuance of treasury bills was discontinued. In March 1934, they again appeared on the domestic scene and sale by auction was introduced.

Although regular bi-weekly auctions began in 1937, there was very little secondary market activity with the bills being acquired almost exclusively by the chartered banks. This began to change in the early to mid-1950s when deliberate steps were taken by monetary officials to establish a purely Canadian money market, including an increase in the amount of treasury bills outstanding and the introduction of a weekly auction.

In 1954 chartered bank day-to-day loans to investment dealers were introduced with one of the effects being to provide investment dealers with an alternate source of funds for financing, among other investments, inventories of federal treasury bills. At the same time the demand for treasury bills was increased further by a revision to the Bank Act which permitted banks to invest more funds in the short-term money market and, naturally, treasury bills were the most attractive form of doing so.

Then in 1955 the chartered banks agreed to maintain a secondary reserve of 7% of their statutory deposits and treasury bills qualified for this reserve.

In recent years the yield-spread between treasury bills and other short-term investments narrowed considerably with the predictable result that a strong secondary market for the bills has developed to the point where they are now the cornerstone of the Canadian short-term money market. The yield on treasury bills is no longer considerably lower than on other short-term investments. But, trying to assess whether treasury bill yields have increased or other yields have decreased is akin to attempting to resolve the age-old chicken and egg controversy.

# Afterword

There you have it. Whether your income is large or small, whether your assets are meagre or substantial, you are bound to be better off if they are managed well. It doesn't really matter where the decimal point falls. You should take charge of your financial affairs and get the most out of your money.

By following the basic rules which are outlined throughout this book, applying a generous dose of common sense, and accepting the fact that you should live within your means, you can make your money count for far more than you ever imagined.

Making your money count is a day-to-day affair. Of course you will need professional help occasionally, but the smarter you get about making your money count, the less that help will cost you and the more beneficial it will become.

In the final analysis the responsibility to get the most for your money falls squarely on your shoulders. Remember, though, it's entirely within your capacity to handle that responsibility. You do not need to be a financier or a chartered accountant to get the most out of your dollar. Just manage it well. Don't read this book and then put it away. Refer to it from time to time as financial decisions need to be made.

# PERSONAL FINANCIAL PLANNING ANALYSIS

FOR _____

This document serves as a starting point, whether used as a check list by the planner or completed by the individual whose affairs are being reviewed. Certain personal questions are omitted because they may best be dealt with in other ways. All lists, schedules and other documents should be attached.

COMPLETED BY _____

DATE _____

## GENERAL INFORMATION

Name in full _____

Home address and telephone _____

_____

_____

Business address and telephone _____

_____

_____

Date of birth _____ Place of birth _____

Citizenship _____

Domicile: at birth _____

        at marriage _____

        at present _____

Marital status _____ Date of marriage _____

Does a marriage contract exist? _____ (if so, attach copy)

State of health _____ Insurable? _____

Do you have a Will? _____ (if so, attach copy)

Executors:

| Name | Relationship to You |
|------|--------------------|
| _____ | _____ |
| _____ | _____ |
| _____ | _____ |
| _____ | _____ |
| _____ | _____ |
| _____ | _____ |

## Address

## SPOUSE

Name in full _____

Home address and telephone (if different from yours) _____

_____

_____

Date of birth _____ Place of birth _____

Citizenship _____ Domicile at marriage _____

Occupation and business address, if any _____

_____

_____

_____

Details of divorce or legal separation, you or your spouse, if any _____

_____

_____

Details of spouse's children, if any, from previous marriage _____

_____

_____

State of health _____

Estimated value and general description of spouse's estate, including source:

_____

_____

_____

_____

Does your spouse have a Will? _____ (if so, attach copy)

## SPOUSE (cont'd)

Executors:

| Name | Relationship to You |
|------|---------------------|
| _____ | _____ |
| _____ | _____ |
| _____ | _____ |
| _____ | _____ |
| _____ | _____ |
| _____ | _____ |

Address

_____

_____

_____

_____

_____

_____

Could your spouse: run a business? _____

handle own affairs? _____

invest funds? _____

Other Comments:

_____

_____

_____

_____

_____

## HEIRS

Complete Schedule II.

Do any of the heirs listed have physical or mental handicaps? If so, give details of any special assistance you may wish to give them.

_____

_____

Do you wish to give any other special assistance to any children, e.g., for education, to set up a business, etc.? If so, give details.

_____

_____

Do you wish to benefit any other persons such as business associates, employees, charities, friends, secret trusts, in-laws, parents or other relatives? If so, give details.

_____

_____

Could any of your children continue your business? _____

_____

_____

How much income will be required for your spouse and children after your death if you:

die before children are independent? _____

die after children are independent but before you retire? _____

die after you retire? _____

If any children have substantial property or income, provide details: ____

_____

_____

_____

## INCOME

Attach a list showing source, type and amount of all of last five years' income (or attach a copy of last five years' income tax returns for both self and spouse).

_____

Indicate any significant changes in income expected in the current or future years:

_____

_____

_____

How much disposable income do you require annually to live at your present standard of living?

_____

_____

_____

Provide details of any settlement, trust, etc., to which you are a party:

_____

_____

_____

_____

_____

Provide details of any substantial gifts or property transfers that you have made at any time:

_____

_____

_____

_____

## INSURANCE, PENSIONS AND OTHER BENEFITS

Complete Schedules III and IV.

Provide details of any other relevant matters: _____

_____

_____

_____

_____

_____

_____

_____

_____

_____

_____

_____

_____

_____

_____

_____

_____

_____

_____

_____

_____

_____

_____

## ASSETS AND LIABILITIES

Complete Schedules V to VII (ignore reference to V-Day values on Schedule VI for assets acquired after 1971).

Have you elected to use V-Day values for capital gains tax purposes?

_____

Complete Schedule VIII and ensure that all obligations are listed, including business and household debts, bank loans, income taxes (including potential liabilities), property taxes, mortgages, notes, etc.

Provide details of any guarantees or endorsements: _____

_____

_____

_____

_____

Complete the following summary using the detailed schedules:

|  | Present Value | Loans Against |
|---|---|---|
| CSV of life insurance | _____ | _____ |
| Current value of pensions | _____ | _____ |
| Current value of real property | _____ | _____ |
| Current value of stocks, etc. | _____ | _____ |
| Other assets | _____ | _____ |
| Other liabilities |  | _____ |
| TOTALS | _____ | _____ |

## OBJECTIVES

At what age would you like to retire? _____

Where will you live when you retire? _____

How much income will you require when retired? _____

Are bequests to be free of death duties?_____

Do you want any special provisions to apply should your spouse remarry?

_____

_____

Are any other bequests to be contingent in any way? If so, give details.

_____

_____

Do you want control of any business to be retained by your estate?

_____

Do you want control of any business to be transferred to any particular person?

_____

Do you want your children to have:

income? _____

capital?_____

capital at a particular age, say 21, 25, etc.?_____

Is there any particular type of investment, business, or hobby in which you are interested, e.g., farming, real estate?

_____

_____

_____

_____

## OTHER COMMENTS

## DOCUMENTS

| | | Attached | To Follow | Not Applicable |
|---|---|---|---|---|
| Schedule I | List of Advisors | ( ) | ( ) | ( ) |
| Schedule II | List of Heirs | ( ) | ( ) | ( ) |
| Schedule III | Summary of Life Insurance | ( ) | ( ) | ( ) |
| Schedule IV | Summary of Pensions, etc. | ( ) | ( ) | ( ) |
| Schedule V | Summary of Real Property | ( ) | ( ) | ( ) |
| Schedule VI | Summary of Stocks, etc. | ( ) | ( ) | ( ) |
| Schedule VII | Other Assets | ( ) | ( ) | ( ) |
| Schedule VIII | Liabilities | ( ) | ( ) | ( ) |
| Last 1 2 3 4 5 years' income tax returns (circle) | | ( ) | ( ) | ( ) |
| Wills – self | | ( ) | ( ) | ( ) |
| – spouse | | ( ) | ( ) | ( ) |

Where are wills kept?

_____

When were they last reviewed?

_____

| | | | | |
|---|---|---|---|---|
| Buy/Sell or partnership agreements | | ( ) | ( ) | ( ) |

Marriage Contract      ( )      ( )      ( )

Other (Indicate)

| | | | |
|---|---|---|---|
| _____ | ( ) | ( ) | ( ) |
| _____ | ( ) | ( ) | ( ) |
| _____ | ( ) | ( ) | ( ) |
| _____ | ( ) | ( ) | ( ) |
| _____ | ( ) | ( ) | ( ) |
| _____ | ( ) | ( ) | ( ) |
| _____ | ( ) | ( ) | ( ) |

**PROFESSIONAL ADVISORS**

**SCHEDULE I**

| | NAME | FIRM | ADDRESS | TELEPHONE NUMBER |
|---|---|---|---|---|
| ACCOUNTANT | | | | |
| LAWYER | | | | |
| BANK MANAGER | | | | |
| LIFE UNDERWRITER | | | | |
| TRUST COMPANY | | | | |
| INVESTMENT COUNSEL | | | | |

**SCHEDULE II**

**HEIRS**  (attach separate lists if necessary)

| NAME AND ADDRESS | RELATIONSHIP | DATE OF BIRTH | MARITAL STATUS | NATURE OF BEQUEST |
|---|---|---|---|---|
|  |  |  |  |  |
|  |  |  |  |  |
|  |  |  |  |  |
|  |  |  |  |  |
|  |  |  |  |  |

**SCHEDULE III**

## SUMMARY OF LIFE INSURANCE

| POLICY NO. | COMPANY | TYPE | FACE AMOUNT | OWNER | BENEFICIARY | ANNUAL PREMIUM | CURRENT CASH VALUE | POLICY LOAN |
|---|---|---|---|---|---|---|---|---|
| | | | | | | | | |
| | | | | | | | | |
| | | | | | | | | |
| | | | | | | | | |
| | | | | | | | | |
| | | | | | | | | |
| | | | | | | | | |
| | | | | | | | | |
| | | | | | | | | |
| TOTALS | | | | | | | | |

COMMENTS: _____

**PENSIONS, ANNUITIES, DISABILITY INSURANCE, ETC.**   **SCHEDULE IV**

| DESCRIPTION | PREMIUMS | BENEFITS | AGE BENEFITS COMMENCE | CURRENT VALUE |
|---|---|---|---|---|
|  |  |  |  |  |
|  |  |  |  |  |
|  |  |  |  |  |
|  |  |  |  |  |
|  |  |  |  |  |
| TOTALS |  |  |  |  |

COMMENTS: _____

_____

_____

**SUMMARY OF REAL PROPERTY**

**SCHEDULE V**

| DESCRIPTION | PURCHASE DATE | COST | V-DAY VALUE | CURRENT VALUE | TYPE OF OWNERSHIP | DETAILS OF MORTGAGE |
|---|---|---|---|---|---|---|
| | | | | | | |
| | | | | | | |
| | | | | | | |
| | | | | | | |
| | | | | | | |
| TOTALS | | | | | | |

# SUMMARY OF STOCKS, BONDS AND MUTUAL FUNDS

**SCHEDULE VI**

| DESCRIPTION | PURCHASE DATE | COST | V-DAY VALUE | CURRENT VALUE | DIVIDEND |
|---|---|---|---|---|---|
| | | | | | |
| | | | | | |
| | | | | | |
| | | | | | |
| | | | | | |
| | | | | | |
| | | | | | |
| | | | | | |
| TOTALS | | | | | |

COMMENTS: _____

**OTHER ASSETS**

**SCHEDULE VII**

| DESCRIPTION AND PURCHASE DATE | COST | V-DAY VALUE | CURRENT VALUE | COMMENTS |
|---|---|---|---|---|
| | | | | |
| | | | | |
| | | | | |
| | | | | |
| | | | | |
| | | | | |
| | | | | |
| | | | | |
| | | | | |
| TOTALS | | | | |

**LIABILITIES**

**SCHEDULE VIII**

| DESCRIPTION | TERM | CURRENT BALANCE | INTEREST RATE | ANNUAL PAYMENTS (INTEREST & PRINCIPAL) | COMMENTS (WHETHER INSURED, ETC.) |
|---|---|---|---|---|---|
| | | | | | |
| | | | | | |
| | | | | | |
| | | | | | |
| | | | | | |
| | | | | | |
| | | | | | |
| TOTALS | | | | | |

# Glossary

Annual Report:
>    The formal financial statements and report on operations
>    presented annually by a corporation to its shareholders after
>    its fiscal year-end.

Averages and Indexes:
>    Statistical tools that theoretically measure the state of the
>    stock market or the economy, based on the performance of
>    stocks or other selected criteria. Well-known indexes and
>    averages include the Dow-Jones Industrial Average, The
>    Toronto Stock Exchange Industrial Index and the Consumer
>    Price Index.

Averaging Down:
>    Buying more of a security at a lower price than your original
>    investment in order to reduce the average cost per unit.

Banking Group:
>    A group of investment houses each of which individually
>    assumes financial responsibility for part of a particular
>    underwriting . *See also "Prospectus"*

Bear:
>    One who expects the market to decline.

Bearer Security:
>    A stock or bond which does not have the owner's name
>    recorded in the books of the issuing company or on the secur-

ity certificate itself and which is therefore payable to the holder. *See also "Street Certificate"*

Bid and Ask:
> A "bid" is the price a prospective buyer is willing to pay; "ask" is the price a seller will accept. The two prices are usually referred to as a "quotation" or a "quote."

Blue Chip:
> Well-established, nationally-known common stocks, usually with a long and satisfactory dividend record and having all the attributes of a safe investment.

Blue Sky Law:
> A slang term for laws enacted to protect the public against securities frauds.

Board Lot:
> A regular trading unit (usually one hundred shares) which has been uniformly decided upon by the stock exchanges.

Board Room:
> A room in a broker's office where clients may watch the quoted prices and sales of listed stocks as shown on a board, usually by means of electronic equipment.

Bond:
> A certificate of indebtedness on which the issuer promises to pay the holder a specified amount of interest for a specified length of time, and to repay the loan on its maturity, and usually implying that assets have been pledged as security for the loan. *See also "Debenture"*

Break-up Value:
> The net amount which would likely be realized upon the winding-up of a business, either upon a voluntary winding-up or a forced liquidation.

Broker:
> An agent who acts for both parties in a transaction.

Bull:
> One who expects the market to rise.

Business Day:
> Any day except Saturday, Sunday and legal holidays.

Buyer's Market:
> When supply exceeds demand.

Call:

A transferable option to buy a specific number of shares at a stated price exercisable over a stated period of time. Obviously, calls would only be purchased by those who expect the subject stock to rise. *See also "Put", "Option"*

Callable:

Redeemable upon due notice by the security's issuer. For example, a corporation might issue bonds which they could pay off and retire upon giving, say, three months notice to the bondholders.

Capital Stock:

The ownership interest in a corporation, evidenced by the issue of share certificates.

Carrying Charges:

Usually refers to interest expense.

Central Bank:

A bank established by a national government to recommend and implement monetary policy on a national-international level. In Canada, it is the Bank of Canada; in the United States, the Federal Reserve Board; in the U.K., the Bank of England.

Certificate:

The actual piece of paper evidencing ownership of a stock or bond.

Closed-end Fund:

An investment company having fixed capital with no provision for the redemption of shares at the option of the shareholder. Shares must be bought or sold on the open market and not through the fund itself. *See "Open-end Fund"*

Collateral Trust Bond:

A bond secured by collateral deposited with a trustee. The collateral is often the stocks and bonds of companies controlled by the issuing company, but may also be other securities.

Commercial Paper:

Short-term, interest-bearing negotiable promissory notes issued by corporations which provide for the payment of a specific amount of money at a stated time.

Common Share:
A synonym for common stock.

Common Stock:
Securities which represent ownership of a corporation and carry with them voting privileges. *See also "Preferred Stock"*

Conglomerate:
A company which directly or indirectly operates in a number of different industries which are usually unrelated to each other.

Consolidated Financial Statements:
The combined financial statements of a parent company and its subsidiaries which present the financial position of the group as if it were one entity.

Consortium:
An association of independent organizations usually formed to undertake a specific project requiring special skills and resources not possessed by any of the participants individually.

Conventional Mortgage:
A mortgage which is not covered by a government-insured program.

Convertible:
A bond, debenture or preferred share which may be exchanged by its owner for common stock of the same company, in accordance with specific terms of the conversion privilege.

Coupon:
That portion of a bond certificate which entitles the holder to an interest payment of a specified amount, when clipped and presented to a paying agent (e.g. a bank) on or after its due date.

Cum Dividend:
A quoted price which includes a declared but unpaid dividend. If one buys a share quoted cum dividend, he will receive the already declared dividend when it is paid. *See pp. 138-9; see also "Ex Dividend"*

Cum Rights:
Shares owned from the day of an announcement that rights are to be issued until the date set for the shares to be traded

"ex-rights" (that is, when the rights and shares will trade separately). The owner of the shares in this period is entitled to receive the rights. *See p. 142; see also "Rights"*

Cumulative Preferred:

A preferred stock having a provision that if one or more of its dividends are not paid they accumulate and are added to the dividends which the preferred shareholders are entitled to in the future.

Current Yield:

The annual income from a particular investment expressed as a percentage of the investment's current value. For example, if income is $100 a year on an investment with a value of $1,000, the current yield is 10%.

Cyclical Stock:

A share in a corporation operating in an industry particularly sensitive to swings in economic conditions.

Day Order:

An order to buy or sell a security valid only for the day on which the order is given.

Debenture:

A certificate of indebtedness of a government or company, usually implying an unsecured obligation. *See also "Bond"*

Delivery, Regular:

Unless otherwise stipulated, those who sell securities must deliver the certificates on or before the fifth business day after the sale.

Discount:

The amount by which a security sells below its par value.

Discretionary Account:

An account established by a customer with a broker under which a representative of the brokerage house has been specifically authorized in writing by the client to use his or her own judgment in buying and selling securities for the account of the customer.

Discretionary Order:

An order given to a broker by a customer specifying the security and the quantity to be bought or sold, but leaving entirely to the judgment of the broker the time and the price of the particular transaction.

Diversified Company:
> A corporation engaged in a number of different lines of business either directly or through subsidiary companies.

Dividend:
> Profits distributed to shareholders of a corporation.

Dow Jones Averages:
> Stock price averages computed by Dow Jones & Company, who also publish the *Wall Street Journal*, giving average stock prices by class based on the highest, lowest, opening, and closing stock price averages for representative share issues. The most commonly used average is that of thirty particular industrial stocks which are listed on the New York Stock Exchange, known as the Dow Jones Industrial.

Earnings Per Share:
> A corporation's earnings for a fiscal period divided by the number of shares outstanding at the end of the particular period which are entitled to full participation in those earnings.

Equity (Shareholders' Equity):
> The ownership interest of common and preferred stockholders in a company, which is the difference between the company's assets and liabilities. If there are only common shares outstanding, "equity per share" would be assets minus liabilities divided by the number of shares outstanding. If there are preferred shares outstanding, it would be assets minus the total of liabilities and par value of preferred shares divided by the number of common shares outstanding.

Escrowed Shares:
> Outstanding shares of a company which, although entitled to vote and receive dividends, cannot be bought or sold without special approval being obtained. Shares can be released from escrow only with the permission of relevant authorities such as the stock exchange or a securities commission. This is a technique commonly used by mining and oil and gas companies when treasury shares are issued for new properties.

Ex Dividend:
> A quoted price which does not include a declared but unpaid dividend. When a person buys a share "ex dividend," he is not entitled to receive the declared but unpaid dividend. It will be paid to the seller of the stock. *See also "Cum Dividend"*

Ex Rights:
> Without rights. The opposite of cum rights. *See also "Cum Rights"*

Extendible Bond:
> A bond issued with a specific maturity date, but granting the holder the right to retain the bond for a specified additional period of time.

Extra:
> Short for extra dividend. A dividend paid in addition to a regular dividend.

Face Value:
> The value of a bond or preferred share appearing on the face of the certificate, usually the amount the issuing company promises to pay at maturity. It is no indication of market value.

Firm Bid:
> An undertaking to buy a specified amount of securities at a stated price for a stated period of time, unless released from the obligation by the potential seller.

Flat:
> A term meaning that the quoted market price of a bond or debenture is the total cost thereof.

Floor Trader:
> An employee of a member firm of a stock exchange who executes buy and sell orders on the floor (trading area) of the exchange on behalf of his firm and its clients.

General Mortgage Bond:
> A bond secured by a blanket mortgage on the issuer's property, but usually outranked by one or more other mortgages.

GTC Order:
> Good-till-cancelled order. Same as an open order.

Growth Stock:
> Shares of a company with excellent prospects for future increases in value.

Hypothecate:
> To pledge as collateral for a loan.

Income Bond or Debenture:
> A bond or debenture which promises to repay principal, but to pay interest only if sufficient income is earned.

Insider:

> A director or senior officer of a corporation, or anyone who may be presumed to have access to inside information concerning the company. Anyone owning more than 10% of the voting shares in a corporation would likely be considered an insider in most jurisdictions.

Insider Report:

> A report of all transactions in the shares of a corporation by those considered to be insiders of the company and submitted on a timely basis to the relevant securities commission.

Institutional Investor:

> An institution, such as a pension fund, trust company or insurance company, which invests large sums of money in securities.

Investment Counsellor:

> One whose profession is giving advice on investments for a fee.

Investment Company, Fund or Trust:

> An organization which uses its capital to invest in other organizations. There are two principal types: closed-end and open-end, the latter usually referred to as mutual funds. *See also "Closed-end Fund" and "Open-end Fund"*

Junior Security:

> A security having a lower priority of claims than another security of the same issuer.

Leading Indicators:

> A selection of statistical data that indicate trends in the economy as a whole. Examples are levels of employment, capital investment, business starts and failures, profits, stock prices, inventories, housing starts and some commodity prices.

Leverage:

> The borrowing and re-investing of money to produce a return in excess of the cost of borrowing.

Limit Order:

> A customer's order to a broker to buy or sell at a stated price or higher. The order can be executed only at the stated, or a higher, price.

Listed Securities:

> Securities which are listed on a stock exchange.

Long:
> Signifies ownership of securities. If you are "long 100 shares of Bell common" it means you own 100 Bell common shares. *See also "Short"*

Margin:
> The amount paid by a customer to a broker when he buys securities on credit, the balance being advanced by the broker against acceptable collateral.

Market Order:
> An order placed to buy or sell a security immediately at the best price obtainable.

Marketable Security:
> A security that can be easily sold.

Mutual Fund:
> An open-end investment company which sells units or shares to investors. The mutual fund uses the proceeds of such sales for itself to invest in securities of various companies and governments. *See also "Open-end Fund"*

Net Worth:
> A synonym for shareholders' equity.

No Par Value Stock:
> Shares which have no par value. Most common shares are issued as having no par value because they are usually bought and sold based on their market value, which reflects supply and demand; and if the company is wound up the common shareholders get everything that's left after all liabilities and preferred shareholders are paid off. *See also "Par Value"*

Odd Lot:
> A number of shares less than the established board lot. *See also "Board Lot"*

Open-end Fund:
> A synonym for a mutual fund. The opposite of a closed-end fund. Open-end funds sell their own shares to investors, buy back their own shares, and are not listed on a stock exchange. The capitalization of an open-end fund is not fixed. It will sell as many shares as people want to buy. *See also "Closed-end Fund" and "Mutual Fund"*

Option:
> A right to buy or sell specific securities at a stated price within a specified period of time.

Over-the-counter:
> Transactions in securities which are not listed on a stock exchange.

Paper Profit:
> An unrealized profit. For example, when a stock purchased at $10 goes up to $15 but has not been sold.

Par Value:
> The face value of a security. This is the amount which the holder is entitled to receive upon redemption of the security by the issuer. It is primarily used in connection with preferred shares and bonds. A preferred share or bond with a par value of $100 would result in the holder thereof receiving $100 on its redemption. The par value is not representative of the security's market value, except immediately before redemption. Some common shares have par values assigned to them, but the par value of a common stock is meaningless, as described previously under "no par value."

Participating Stock:
> A class of preferred stock which provides for payment of a dividend not less than that paid on the company's common shares. Occasionally, a participating stock will also share in the residual distribution of assets upon liquidation of a corporation.

Penny Stock:
> Low-priced, speculative issues selling at less than $1 a share. Usually used as a derogatory term, even though some penny stocks develop into investment-calibre issues.

Point:
> As applied to the price of shares, it means $1 per share. For bonds, is usually means 1% of the face value. If a stock goes up or down 2½ points, that means the price has increased or decreased by $2.50 per share. A $1,000 bond that dropped 2 points would have gone down in value by $20.

Portfolio Investments:
> Long-term investments in corporations which are neither subsidiaries nor controlled by the investor.

Preferred Stock:
>A class of share capital that entitles the holder to certain preferences over common shareholders, such as a fixed rate of dividend, or return of the stock's par value upon liquidation, or both. Preferred shares normally have voting rights only when their dividends are in arrears.

Premium:
>The amount by which a preferred stock or bond sells above its par value. In the case of a new issue of bonds or stocks, the premium is the amount the market price rises over the original selling price. The term may also refer to that part of the redemption price of a bond or preferred stock in excess of par.

Price-earnings Ratio:
>The market price of a common stock dividend by the annual earnings per share for the preceding fiscal period.

Primary Distribution or Primary Offering:
>The original sale of any issue of a corporation's securities.

Private Sector:
>The sector of an economy consisting of individuals, corporations, firms and other institutions not under government control.

Profit Taking:
>The process of converting paper profits into cash by selling the securities.

Pro Forma:
>For illustrative purposes.

Prospectus:
>A legal document describing securities being offered for sale to the public. A prospectus must be prepared in conformity with the requirements of the securities commissions in jurisdictions where the securities will be offered for sale.

Proxy:
>A written authorization given by a shareholder to another person (who need not be a shareholder) to represent the shareholder and vote the shareholder's shares at a shareholders' meeting.

Proxy Battle:
>A contest between two or more factions in a corporation in which each faction seeks to gain control of sufficient proxies

to enable it to elect its candidates to the board of directors or win a decision in a particular vote at a shareholders' meeting.

Public Company:

A corporation whose shares are available to the general public.

Public Sector:

The sector of an economy consisting of government-owned institutions.

Put:

A transferable option to sell a specific number of shares at a stated price exercisable over a stated period of time. Puts are purchased by those who think a stock is going to go down. *See also "Calls"*

Rally:

A brisk rise following a decline in the general price level of the market as a whole or of an individual stock.

Record Date:

The date on which a shareholder must be registered on a corporation's books in order to receive a dividend declared or to vote on the company's affairs.

Red Herring:

A preliminary prospectus, so-called because certain information is printed in red ink around the border of the front page. A red herring will not contain all the information found in the final prospectus. Its purpose is to determine the extent of public interest in a new security issue while it is being reviewed by the relevant securities commission.

Retractable Share:

A share having a fixed maturity date at a fixed price, at the option of the investor.

Rights:

Privileges granted to shareholders enabling them to acquire additional shares directly from the company.

Secondary Distribution or Secondary Offering:

The re-distribution to the public of a significant number of shares which had previously been sold by the issuing company.

Seller's Market:

When demand exceeds supply.

Senior Debt:
> Debt having a higher priority of claims than other debt.

Senior Security:
> A security having a higher priority of claims than other securities.

Settlement Date:
> The date on which stock exchange transactions are due for delivery and payment. It is also the official date to be used for recording stock market transactions for income tax purposes. It is usually the fifth business day following the date of the transaction.

Shareholder of Record:
> The shareholder in whose name shares are registered in the records of a corporation.

Shareholders' Equity:
> The excess of assets over liabilities of a corporation.

Short:
> Signifies that securities have been sold on your behalf, but you still haven't delivered them to your broker. *See also "Short Sale"*

Short Sale:
> The sale of a security which the seller doesn't own. It is a highly speculative transaction done in anticipation of the price of a stock falling and the seller then being able to cover the sale of buying the stock later at a lower price, thereby making a profit on the transaction. It is an offence for a seller not to advise his broker that a sale is "short."

Stock Dividend:
> A dividend paid by the issue of shares of capital stock rather than in cash.

Stock Option:
> The right to purchase a stated number of shares of a corporation's capital stock at a fixed price at or during a fixed period of time. Such rights are usually given to officers and employees of the corporation.

Stock Split:
> The division of the outstanding shares of a corporation into a larger number of shares without a change in value of the total shares outstanding. For example, one $500 share might be replaced by fifty shares each worth $10.

Stop-loss Order:
>   An order for the sale of securities designed to take effect as
>   soon as the market price of the security reaches a specified
>   amount.

Street Certificate:
>   A stock certificate registered in the name of an investment
>   dealer rather than in the name of the individual owner. This
>   situation makes it easier to transact sales and purchases of
>   the particular shares.

Subsidiary:
>   A corporation in which another corporation owns a majority
>   of the voting shares.

Takeover Bid:
>   A bid to purchase shares of a corporation with a view to
>   obtaining control of the corporation.

Treasury Stock or Treasury Shares:
>   Authorized but unissued shares.

Underwriting:
>   The term applied to the agreement by investment dealers to
>   buy, at an agreed price, all of the issue of a securities offer.
>   The investment dealer will then sell the securities to the gen-
>   eral public.

Warrant:
>   A certificate giving the holder the right to purchase securities
>   at a stated price within a stated period of time.

Wash Sale:
>   A sale which is immediately offset by an identical purchase.

# Index